THE
PERFECT
LIFE

THE
PERFECT
LIFE

The Shakers in America

Doris Faber

Farrar, Straus and Giroux   New York

Library of Congress Cataloging in Publication Data
Faber, Doris, 1924–
The perfect life: the Shakers in America.
Bibliography: p.
1.   Shakers—United States—Juvenile literature.
[1.   Shakers]   I.   Title.
BX9766.F3   289.8′0973   73-90968
ISBN 0-374-35819-2

First printing, 1974

PRINTED IN THE UNITED STATES OF AMERICA
Published simultaneously in Canada
by Doubleday Canada Ltd., Toronto

Designed by Sheila Lynch

ACKNOWLEDGMENTS

In gathering the material upon which this book is based, I received much friendly help from many different quarters. Among those to whom I am particularly indebted are Robert F. W. Meader, director of the Shaker Museum at Old Chatham, New York, and his entire staff, especially Mrs. Claire Wheeler, who has charge of the museum's library; besides noting my gratitude for being allowed to use this extensive collection, I must acknowledge my thanks for permission to quote numerous brief passages in the pages that follow. Similarly, I must also thank Sister Mildred Barker of the Sabbathday Lake Shaker Community for letting me intrude on the community's privacy; and Theodore Johnson, director of the library at Sabbathday, for his generosity in permitting me to study the rare old volumes relating to Mother Ann Lee's English background that he collected in the course of his own research in Manchester. Others whose assistance I must mention include Mrs. Lawrence K. Miller, president of the Hancock Shaker Community; Mrs. Mary Alm of the Pine Plains Library, who secured the loan of various hard-to-find old books through the resources of Mid-Hudson Libraries; and also many staff members in the reference department and in the manuscript room of the New York State Library in Albany who were always patient and helpful when I called upon them for guidance while investigating the comprehensive Shaker collection there. Above all, I would like to thank Elizabeth Gordon for inspiring the writing of this book.

D.F.

Contents

THE
PERFECT
LIFE

❦ *One* ❦

"Oh, the letters!"

A BRIGHT OCTOBER SUN is warming the crisp Maine air outside, but only seven of the forty-eight rooms in this old building are centrally heated and Sister Mildred Barker's office is not one of them. Sitting there, I feel cold.

The frost that had whitened the ground a few hours earlier surely accounts for the chill, or does it? With each passing minute, my doubts increase. Nevertheless, an opportunity that might not be repeated must be taken advantage of, and I doggedly ask questions about the daily routine followed by the handful of Shakers still living here at Sabbathday Lake.

A faint smile suddenly appears on Sister Mildred's face. "There was an editor of *Rolling Stone* who came up last Thursday," she says unexpectedly. "He wanted to know exactly the same things."

Nobody has tinkered with the smoldering black-iron stove in the corner, but all at once the room seems much warmer. For Sister Mildred's remark explains a small mystery that should have been clear right from the beginning. No wonder her welcome has been so restrained.

3

This is one of just two surviving Shaker communities, from an original total of nineteen. Except for Canterbury in neighboring New Hampshire, the others were all abandoned when their dwindling membership could no longer maintain them, and even Canterbury has been reduced to a tiny company of elderly, ailing members who decline to see most would-be interviewers. Yet Shakerism has become increasingly popular during recent years—so the brunt of the world's demands must fall upon Sister Mildred and the other Shakers at Sabbathday Lake.

In times past, the remoteness of the Sabbathday colony had protected it from worldly scrutiny. But now its back road is hardly more than an hour's drive from a jetport, and clumps of vacation cottages are creeping ever closer. Among the few sisters remaining here, the one appointed to take charge of the community's business with outsiders must be constantly harried these days.

Having had some idea about all this, I had waited purposely until October before troubling Sister Mildred. From the pages of *The Shaker Quarterly*, published at Sabbathday for research libraries and collectors of Shaker lore, I had gathered that the summer tourist season put quite a strain on the community's limited resources. However, the thought that the autumn might be almost as busy had simply not occurred to me when I wrote a letter requesting permission to come then.

The letter had informed Sister Mildred that a book about the Shakers was being planned—a book addressed to a new generation seeking many of the same goals that had motivated the most successful experiment in communal living in America's history. Surely a worthy project like this justified intruding on the privacy of Sabbathday's residents, the letter had implied.

Remembering its contents, I am forced to smile wryly. Of course, the man from *Rolling Stone* had also convinced himself that conscientious research required a firsthand inspection of the Shaker settlement up in Maine. So, doubtless, had assorted antique dealers and collectors. Not to mention youthful enthusiasts interested in communal living, or students assigned a term paper on some Shaker topic.

But the truth, which Sister Mildred must know better than anybody else, is that research material about the Shakers can be found easily in specialized libraries and museums. There are detailed diaries by Shakers themselves and reports by outsiders of every possible bias which illuminate earlier periods in the Shaker experience. Actual Shaker dwellings, barns, and workshops have been preserved. More Shaker tools and furniture and other artifacts are available for careful study than even the most diligent students would need to arrive at valid conclusions about the Shaker culture of the eighteenth and nineteenth centuries. As for Shakerism today, it is readily apparent that a declining population has long since halted most traditional Shaker activities. Those few Shakers who have remained faithful can scarcely give as reliable opinions about the reasons for the decline as more impartial historians.

There is only one area where Shakers might be expected to speak with greater authority than any stranger: the deeply personal matter of the inner meaning of Shakerism. And even here, *The Shaker Quarterly* has already provided many thoughtful statements. Among these, Sister Mildred's own contemporary testimony offers all the serious re-searcher should require:

> Once, many years ago, Mother Ann admonished her followers, "Do all your work as though it were to last a thousand years and you were to die tomorrow." With these words she gave us both the basic essence of Shaker-ism itself as well as a key to understanding all of those things which would in the normal course of events grow out of the movement.
>
> We see here readily that all the Shaker does, is done under the shadow of eternity. . . .

What purpose, then, can be served by insisting on visiting Sabbathday? Facing Sister Mildred's watchful gaze with some discomfort, I am ready now to admit the answer. Curiosity, pure and simple, has inspired this trip. At practically no other place on earth is it still possible to see a real live Shaker.

Impulsively I suppose aloud that it must be terribly upsetting to be peered at constantly and prodded with innumerable questions. Sister Mildred nods gratefully. "You begin to feel like some kind of a freak," she says.

In fact, Sister Mildred's appearance is far from singular. Once all Shaker women had worn drab long dresses, and caps or bonnets covering their hair completely; the men had their own rather old-fashioned peasant costume. But Sister Mildred is wearing an ordinary sweater with a skirt of the same length that many women in their middle years commonly wear, and her graying hair is pulled back into a neat bun. Indeed, in any other setting besides this vestige of the Shaker past, nobody would think of staring at her. Even here, the simple words she has just spoken sound so normal that there is no longer a tension in the air.

Or perhaps the fire in the old iron stove has finally

caught hold, for the room now seems quite comfortable. And instead of being impatient to start exploring the rest of the building, I have begun to think an unsuspected discovery might be made right here. In at least one respect the last of the Shakers are no different from the first, because the aim of Shakerism has never changed.

To live *the perfect life*. That was the ideal adopted by the sect's founders two centuries ago, during the same years that saw the founding of the United States. The temper of those days was epitomized by the horsewhippings that occurred when a small band of religious separatists had dared to claim such a seemingly ridiculous goal. Over the two hundred years of swiftly increasing and then gradually decreasing Shaker vigor, the outer world's grudging tolerance had slowly yielded to admiration. Now, in the 1970's, about the same number of Shakers were striving to live the perfect life as had started the movement back when the Declaration of Independence was first being proposed. And what was the main difficulty confronting today's believers?

"Oh, the letters!" Sister Mildred exclaims. "More and more and more keep coming." Most of them are written by students from junior high to graduate school, and they usually request staggering amounts of information. With a suddenly shrill voice, Sister Mildred mockingly recites a typical letter: "My paper is due next Monday, so will you please send me complete details immediately . . ."

In her own gentler tone, she says that she wishes it were possible to reply fully to such mail, for the Shakers have always felt an obligation to tell the world all it wanted to know about Shakerism. "But we don't have a staff to do that work," she explains.

7

While she has been speaking, a large man wearing a blue sweater and slacks has entered the room, and Sister Mildred now introduces him as Theodore Johnson, the director of the Shaker Library at Sabbathday. "He's the main staff," she adds.

Mr. Johnson amiably accepts the description, but his tone is less good-humored as he proceeds to list the kinds of calls for help that increasingly consume his time. Photographers. Candlemakers. Interior decorators. They all demand hours of personal attention. Either they ask questions that require an exhaustive search through old ledgers and other documents for an answer, or they want to disrupt the whole community by doing the searching themselves. They do not seem to realize that this is not a museum or a richly endowed library with facilities for offering such services, Mr. Johnson says sternly. But what upsets him more is that most outsiders also do not realize that this is a living community—the home of people who put a special value on preserving their privacy. Particularly in the summer, when a few guides are available to escort visitors around specified areas, someone is always straying into the living quarters, so the residents must be constantly alert for prying eyes. And for light fingers, too, because Shaker furnishings have recently been bringing fabulous prices at antique sales— such as $250 for a plain wooden Shaker coat hanger. Under these circumstances, no outsider can be allowed to wander anywhere on the property alone. Mr. Johnson smiles to ease the strictness of his last statement.

Sister Mildred has been listening approvingly. Now, with a brisk nod, she gets up and leaves the room, closing the door after her. I can only hope she will return, but meanwhile Mr. Johnson seems disposed to continue the conversation. No, he is not a Shaker, he willingly explains, although he would very much like to become one. However, the last new member had been admitted in 1953, and since then a decision he cannot support has decreed the end of all further recruiting. Pressed for more details, he chooses his words carefully.

He would not want to provoke any controversy, he notes, but there is some difference of opinion within the Shaker family. Until 1947, he recalls, the ministry at the Shaker community in Mount Lebanon, New York, had been accepted by every Shaker as the supreme authority on all major questions. After Mount Lebanon and then another nearby colony had been obliged to shut down, Canterbury in New Hampshire had assumed the role of directing policy. It was Canterbury that had decided there could be no more Shakers. Sabbathday regrets this, Mr. Johnson says, but preserving Shaker harmony is more important than raising any public protest.

As he is completing his explanation, the door opens again and Sister Mildred announces that lunch will be ready any minute. She rather brusquely invites me to join them in the dining room. As I hesitate, feeling that I should impose no further, Sister Mildred repeats her invitation more warmly, and I am delighted to accept.

The wide hallway we cross is dim and unheated, but the varnished wood of the floors and door frames gives it a pleasing mellow quality. Within the dining room, the polish of half a dozen long cherry-wood tables ranged in parallel rows reinforces the same impression. I try to imagine the scene a hundred years ago—when there would have been a soundless parade of Shaker men marching in at one end of the room, and of Shaker women at the other, all approaching their assigned tables, where they would stop and kneel in silent prayer before taking their seats. The contrast between the Shaker past and present suddenly seems unutterably sad.

For now there are hardly more than half a dozen people unceremoniously taking places at the only table that has been set with silverware. Even this small group includes several guests, among them the wife of the farmer who has been renting the Shakers' apple orchard in recent years. Apparently, several of the remaining sisters prefer for one reason or another to have this meal separately.

Still the atmosphere is quite cheerful, and I soon find myself relaxing as friendly chatter dispels musings about the past. Then a sturdy woman introduced as Sister Frances, who is currently in charge of kitchen chores under the traditional Shaker practice of rotating duties, brings in two steaming tureens. Her method of serving the soup is another reminder of the Shaker heritage. To simplify mealtime procedure, the early Shakers had made each seated square of four people the unit of their planning—for every four persons they set out a platter of whatever food had been prepared, so everybody along the long tables could conveniently help himself.

The tomato soup itself is of special interest. No ordinary canned variety, it has obviously been created from a Shaker recipe blending a flavorful broth with spicy bits of whole tomato. However, the tuna-fish sandwiches that follow are in no way remarkable, even the bread being store-bought. Although homemade cookies with fresh fruit salad for dessert somewhat redeem the main course, I am privately a little disappointed by the meal. In the old days, Shakers reputedly ate very well indeed, and recently several Shaker cookbooks have been published by commercial publishing houses. But then, how could such a small community, no longer able to operate its own farm, be compared to the thriving agricultural village that had once supplied abundant fresh produce for all the tables here?

While I was thinking this, Sister Mildred had excused herself to answer a telephone in the kitchen. Now she returns, nodding her head disbelievingly. "That was a teacher of weaving," she reports. The teacher had wanted to come up to Maine on Monday to see a complete collection of the early Shaker weaving patterns. Today was Saturday, and tomorrow would be the Sabbath. Yet this woman had thought she was giving enough advance notice, when it would take at least two weeks to assemble what she was asking for—if anybody could be spared from regular duties for that amount of time. Sister Mildred sighs deeply as she concludes this recital.

In addition to Sister Mildred and Sister Frances, I have by now made the acquaintance of the two other sisters at the dining table. They are both vigorous women approaching old age but looking entirely capable of carrying out routine housekeeping chores. However, the house they are obliged to keep is this enormous, drafty structure designed to accommodate around a hundred people. Back when half of the building had been occupied by the Shaker brothers who farmed or made furniture or did other heavy work, there had been dozens of Shaker sisters to take their turn at cooking or cleaning and the like. The last Shaker brother here had died in 1961, and although the smaller Shaker family required fewer tasks to maintain itself, it still had to care for the community's extensive land holdings and somehow pay its necessary expenses. How were ten aging women possibly accomplishing all this?

With some realization now of what the answer must be, I repeat an earlier question. Could Sister Mildred describe the way each member of the community had spent the morning? But before the sister can reply, she is summoned once more to the telephone and Mr. Johnson answers for her. He concentrates a moment, then counting on his fingers, lists the after-breakfast activity of each member of the community:

SISTER MILDRED drove to the post office to pick up the mail.

Sister Frances was in the kitchen.

Sister Elizabeth was pushing a mop around the corridors.

Sister Elsie was out in the workshop sewing away at aprons to be sold in the little store beside the road.

Sister Minnie was probably working on potholders.

Sister Della was also sewing in the workshop.

Sister Marie was looking after Sister Eleanor, who had recently suffered a heart attack.

Sister Gertrude was helping over at Canterbury, where the average age of the remaining sisters was eighty-eight.

Sister Ethel was in a nursing home.

When Mr. Johnson finishes, I sit a moment hesitating. Apparently only half of the sisters here at Sabbathday are still strong enough to do much work—and with all the pressures the world keeps inflicting on them, how can they carry on? Under such difficult circumstances, what gives them the strength to continue seeking the perfect life?

In many ways, their lot is really no easier than that of

the first Shakers who faced outright persecution. Yet before I can put the thought in words, a part of the reason for their fortitude becomes apparent. Sister Frances, hurrying in from the kitchen, reports that a "hippie" has just arrived at the back door. With his wife and baby, or at least she supposes they are married. I am startled by the sister's remark, because Shakers have always been noted for their strict moral standards. When Sister Frances adds that she is giving the new arrivals some lunch, I blurt a question: Isn't it hard for a Shaker to accept people whose code of behavior is so different from their own? Sister Frances laughs heartily, as if she is accustomed to enjoying good jokes. "I think it's rather flattering," she says, "that they think we'll accept them."

Sister Mildred, who has also returned from the kitchen, appears less amused. Most of these people who say they are interested in communal life are only interested until they try it, she observes tartly. Again she shows her talent as a mimic: "We just want to spend the day with you so we can learn from you!" But spending a day here will not be much help, Sister Mildred says, seemingly still talking about the would-be commune dwellers. They do not realize it's not merely a question of coming together and loving each other, she goes on, they don't know what it costs to bring this about.

"There is something in back of what they see," Sister Mildred says firmly.

She is quite right, I agree. To find out what is truly behind the Shaker belief, it is necessary to look beyond the Maine village of Sabbathday—back to the grimy industrial town of Manchester in England in the early 1700's.

Two

Toad Lane

IT WAS SCARCELY TWO HUNDRED PACES from the cathedral square, but it might almost have beeen a different world. The mud, the noise, the smells of Toad Lane would certainly have caused any fine lady to wrinkle her nose with disgust—if the wife or daughter of a rich mill owner had ever ventured there. Whole families were crowded into filthy little rooms, disease was rampant and the infant death rate high. No wonder despairing mothers and fathers sought to forget their misery by drinking themselves senseless at one of the numerous grog shops along the narrow roadway.

For Ann Lee, the daughter of a Toad Lane blacksmith, each day brought new shudders of horror. She was an unusually sensitive girl who turned toward religion when she was still very young. This much is known about her, but only by her own testimony many years later. On Toad Lane, it was unlikely that even the birth date of an infant would be recorded, and hers was not. According to oral tradition, though, Ann Lee is supposed to have been born on February 28, 1736.

Otherwise, little is known about her early existence except that she was probably the second of eight children in the family of one John Lee or Lees. Some entries in a musty register of baptisms point toward this conclusion. There are no further clues. Considering that reading and writing were rare skills among the common people of Manchester then—skills which Ann herself never learned—the lack of evidence is hardly surprising.

Nor is it surprising that she apparently went to work even before she entered her teens. Since 1350, when some Flemish weavers had been allowed to settle in the area, Manchester had become noted as a textile center. Although the well-known local cloth was originally woven on cottage looms, by Ann's time the Industrial Revolution had already wrought great changes in what had once been a peaceful village set amid green fields.

Now new machines were speeding up the process of clothmaking, and factories were replacing home labor. Hoping to improve their lot, poor folk from the surrounding countryside flocked to the town, further crowding old neighborhoods like Toad Lane or filling row on row of shoddy new houses mushrooming in every direction. "It is said," a history of the town relates, "that no fewer than two thousand new houses were built in the Manchester area between 1719 and 1739." The population approximately doubled during this period, totaling around 20,000. Although London had the incredible population of 700,000, some travelers thought Manchester might soon rival it. Yet even if Manchester was growing so rapidly, only a small portion of its citizens enjoyed the town's increasing prosperity.

While the owners of textile mills were amassing huge

fortunes, the working people suffered more every year. For each new invention had the effect of reducing the number of experienced artisans whose talents were needed. Although the expanding industry did indeed provide additional jobs, most of these required no special skills, and shrewd businessmen saw no sense in paying a penny above the lowest wage for this kind of help. The result was that whole families had to toil from dawn till dark, or else face starvation.

So Ann Lee merely shared the common lot when—as she later recalled—she spent much of her girlhood cutting velvet or cotton threads. What set her apart, though, was the intensity of her feeling that life must have some higher purpose than the mean struggle she noted on every side. Among her acquaintances, she undoubtedly heard mutterings of the protests against the factory system that would erupt into riots within a few decades. But her own bent toward religion made her look for hope in a different direction.

The old stone cathedral not far from Toad Lane offered little comfort to a deeply emotional girl like Ann. Having weathered years of ferment, when battles were fought about religious issues and jails were filled with people who dared to dispute the authority of England's official church, the clergy in Manchester as well as in the rest of the country had become accustomed to a sedate form of worship. The services they conducted lacked the fire of an earlier day. To a girl who often sat up all night convulsed with tears because of the sin she saw everywhere, something much stronger was necessary if she were to find peace.

Had she been able to escape the squalor of Toad Lane, Ann's keen mind might have given her other outlets for her emotions. Although in Manchester making money seemed to be the most important human aim, stirrings of new values were already being felt. In the year that Ann turned twenty, the town's first circulating library was founded. And for two years before that, the town's first daily newspaper, *The Manchester Mercury*, had been broadening the horizon of its subscribers.

Edited by a Mrs. Raffald, who had apparently come from London, the paper encouraged local cultural developments. Describing a performance in Manchester's new theater entitled "Harlequin Sorcerer," Mrs. Raffald wrote, "In the Language of the Town, I might say tis a very pretty thing, mighty pretty, exceedingly pretty, and all that; But in the exact critical idiom I must pronounce it to be great, magnifique, and surprising." Even foreign news was provided, whenever letters were received from abroad, as for instance:

Swedish Finland Dec. 16, 1752
Shocks of an Earthquake were felt here, accompanied with a great Noise, and a Smell of Sulphur arising out of the Ground. The 21st another Shock was felt but neither of them did any considerable Damage. This Phenomenon being very rare in these Northern Countries, gives the Inhabitants some Uneasiness.

But Ann Lee's environment had permitted no possibility of her learning to read, so all such distractions were denied to her. Instead she kept sinking deeper into despair, until when she was twenty-two she met a tailor and his wife, James and Jane Wardley. They, too, had been searching for a religious answer to the terrible suffering surrounding them and at first had become Quakers.

However, the Wardleys failed to achieve the inner peace that Quakerism, with its emphasis on personal religious experience instead of ceremony, had brought to other dissenters from the established Church of England. Still troubled, the tailor and his wife looked further—and found "the French prophets."

These were a small band of men and women who had been exiled from their homes in the mountains of southern France because of their radical religious ideas. Arriving in London in 1706, they had tried to win English recruits, but most of their efforts had brought them only ridicule. For besides asserting their special gift of predicting the second coming of Christ, which inspired the name the "French prophets," their manner of worship also upset most observers.

A sort of frenzy seemed to possess the believers as they heard what they later insisted had been divine voices. Their arms and legs moved with such peculiar abandon, their own voices shouted such strange sounds, that they were obviously in some kind of trance. In France, they had been given another sarcastic label, Les Trembleurs. The Shakers.

But in England the French prophets attracted so few followers that this name might never have been translated had the Wardleys not come under their spell. By the time this happened, late in the 1740's, the French immigrants themselves had already scattered to other countries, leaving only a tiny nucleus of believers in London. For some reason the Wardleys decided to start a similar group in Manchester, and it was here that Ann Lee began the real work of her life.

She was twenty-two when she joined the Wardley group in 1758. Many years afterward, even those who loved her best could remember no particular mark of destiny that distinguished her from the other ten or a dozen members. She was a young woman of medium height and serious manner, it seems, whose appearance was sufficiently pleasing for some to wonder why she had not married.

Yet if she spoke her mind on the subject at any of their meetings, she must have expressed her belief that marriage was a sinful state. She had already reached this conclusion, possibly because she had seen frightening scenes of sexual violence during her childhood. Despite the teachings of the Bible, she had become convinced that all fleshly relations between men and women were a sin no church ceremony could sanctify.

And sin was the main focus of the Wardley meetings. Doubtless owing to the Wardleys' Quaker past, these meetings would start with a period of silent meditation, lasting until someone present was moved to rise. Soon the whole group would be taken "with a mighty shaking . . . singing, shouting," as the Shakers' own history* of their movement relates, "under which they would express the indignation of God against all sin."

However, at the age of twenty-six, Ann Lee did marry. Her husband, a blacksmith like her father, was Abraham Standerin, or Stanley, according to different entries in the cathedral records. The story of her next four years is briefly told in these church documents, for they note the birth of a baby every year—and then the death of the infant within a few months.

Four such tragedies could not fail to have an effect on any mother. In Ann's case, the immediate effect was a

---

* *Testimonies of the life, character, revelations and doctrines of our ever blessed Mother Ann Lee*, a manuscript compiled from interviews with the early Shakers soon after Mother Ann's death and later printed in several slightly differing versions.

collapse that apparently led to a brief confinement in an insane asylum. This episode, which would give rise to repeated rumors calling her an escaped lunatic, was frequently denied in later years, even though cryptic references in Shaker writings indicate its basis in fact. Nevertheless, there can be no question that the lasting change wrought by the death of Ann's infants was significant.

Any woman who had suffered as Ann had might have concluded that she was being punished for some terrible sin of her own. Because Ann Lee already believed marriage was sinful, it was hardly surprising that she saw the loss of her babies as God's way of punishing her for her personal sin. But her powerful religious fervor made her go still further. From her private anguish, she found a compelling motive for constructing a whole new religion.

Until her searing lesson about God's wrath, Ann Lee had been merely a follower in the Wardley group. The only real bond holding this group together was a shared hatred of sin in any guise. None of the members had been able to offer a positive creed. They knew what they were against, but they lacked a program for redeeming sinners who truly wished they could purge themselves of all evil. Now Ann started to devote her strength to the supreme task of finding such a path, and in the process she inevitably emerged as the group's leader.

At first, her quest was hidden from the world's gaze. "Sometimes I labored all night, continually crying to God for my own redemption," she later told her friends. "My sufferings were so great, that . . . bloody sweat pressed through the pores of my skin, and I became as helpless as an infant. And when I was brought through, and born into the spiritual kingdom, I was like an infant just born into the natural world."

Then the results of her personal struggle became known in wider circles. Despite the magnitude of the spiritual truths she said she was discovering, the uninitiated could scarcely understand how her new kingdom differed from the heaven of other religions. That she appeared to believe heaven was attainable while still on earth was pure nonsense to the ears of conventional believers. Yet the force of Ann's conviction was such that she seemingly swayed not just most of the Wardley group but also some previous skeptics, including her own father and husband.

They listened to her—and they acted with her. The expense ledger kept by the constable of Manchester indicates a bare outline of how they assisted Ann in spreading word of her new gospel at frenzied meetings that struck more traditional worshippers as a dangerous profaning of the Sabbath.

During 1772, the constable noted payment of the following bills:

	Shillings	*Pence*
July 14—To apprehending 5 Shakers on Sunday last, 6 pence each for 24 assistants	12	
To Ale for 24 persons apprehending the Shakers	5	6
July 23—To the Jurors Bailiff on prosecuting John Lees and his Daughter Ann	1	6

July 30—To a Bill of Expenses at the Mule when Justice Mainwaring attended to the examination of the Shakers	2	7½
Oct 10—To Widow Shapley for Ironwork when the Shakers were apprehended	2	6
Oct 19—To repairs making good the breaches at Lees in Toad Lane in order to apprehend a gang of Shakers locked up there	5	2
To sundry persons and expenses Quelling a Mob who were beginning to pull down the House of John Townley, a Shaker	5	6
Oct 30—To Ann Lees a shaker apprehended for disturbing the Congregation in the old church detaining her in the Prison room two days 2 pence and maintaining her with meat and drink	6	3

While the circumstances attending each of these incidents can only be surmised, it seems clear that the small group of Manchester Shakers had offended the general public by their methods of conducting their own services, and even more by their insistence on interfering with the regular services in the town cathedral. Whatever the circumstances, the crucial point for the Manchester authorities

—and for the future history of Shakerism—came just a year later, in the summer of 1773.

Then Ann Lee and four other Shakers were arrested again, for "wilfully and contemptuously" interrupting another cathedral service, as *The Manchester Mercury* reported on July 20. By now, Justice Mainwaring must have been infuriated, for each of the defendants was fined twenty pounds. This was an enormous sum in those days, probably more than $1,000 in terms of modern purchasing power. Nobody could imagine that poor working people would be able to pay such a fine, so the obvious intention of the Justice was that these Shakers should languish in jail until they could be trusted not to cause any more trouble. How the four others who were sentenced with Ann Lee managed to secure their freedom is not mentioned in Shaker annals.

But for Ann Lee herself, the prison stay had a miraculous outcome. The awesome transformation of a Manchester factory girl that took place during the same few weeks gave Shakerism the inspiration for its whole future.

Like the miracles of any religion, the Shaker miracle must be accepted on faith. To a disbeliever, the fact that Ann Lee was confined in a cell with no food or water for fourteen days seems highly unlikely. Even in an eighteenth-century town where "common scolds" were still punished by having an iron band padlocked over their mouth, could starvation really be the penalty for disturbing the peace? And even if such extreme cruelty was sanctioned, could it happen that Ann's particular cell had a keyhole accessible from the street? And that a loyal friend could pour sufficient wine and water through the stem of a pipe to keep Ann alive during her ordeal?

23

These are the simpler sort of questions which can easily —and negatively—be answered by common sense and a study of Manchester's old records. The rest of the Shaker account of Ann Lee's prison experience is totally beyond testing. For the Shakers hold that their leader had a vision while she was in prison, that Jesus Christ appeared to her and revealed the true way to gain salvation. She was so changed by this knowledge that she was no longer human but divine. After she was released from her cell, her fellow Shakers gave full credence to the miracle she related. From then on, they called her Mother Ann.

For the next nine months, the Shakers of Manchester were in a sense waiting to learn how they were to spread the new word they had received. The absence of any additional entries in the constable's expense ledger or on court records suggests they were waiting quietly. In their own history, they tell of living "in almost entire peace," suffering only minor persecutions. Then, at last, they received the sign they had been expecting.

It came, not to Mother Ann herself, but to James Whittaker, the follower who was said to have fed her liquids through a pipe stem during her imprisonment. Now a young man of twenty-three, James had been a devoted Shaker for several years. So no one was surprised when he reported seeing a vision of his own as he stopped by the side of the road to eat on his way to a meeting one Saturday evening.

"While I was sitting there," he told his friends, "I saw a vision of America, and I saw a large tree, and every leaf thereof shone with such brightness as made it appear like a burning torch."

The meaning of James Whittaker's sign was perfectly clear to Mother Ann. She immediately sent another of her followers to the seaport of Liverpool. There he secured passage for a small party of Shakers aboard a ship called the *Mariah*, which was bound for New York.

❦ *Three* ❦

Niskayuna

DOCKSIDE GOSSIP in Liverpool had it that the *Mariah* was
no longer really seaworthy. John Hocknell, the Manchester
Shaker who had been sent to see about booking passage, had dutifully told Mother Ann that people were
saying the ship was destined to sink. "I told him," she later
related, "that God would not condemn it when we were
in it."

So she confidently led her party aboard on May 10, 1774.
Besides Mother Ann and the man who still considered himself her husband even though she denied the relationship,
there were only six others. These included a brother and a
niece of Ann's, another woman named Mary Partington,
James Whittaker, and also John Hocknell and his son
Richard. Hocknell's savings from the shop he had kept paid
the expenses of the whole group. Possibly he had been
unable to provide for a larger number, or perhaps the
Wardleys and the rest of the original Shakers had their own
reasons for not wanting to uproot themselves. In any case,
their commitment to Shakerism did not survive Mother
Ann's departure, nothing further being heard of them.

But the eight who did embark felt their religion so strongly that Captain Smith of the *Mariah* soon was sorry he had accepted them as passengers. Having been warned beforehand that the Shakers had been great troublemakers in Manchester, conducting themselves like raving lunatics during what they called their worship services, Captain Smith had at first refused to take them. Then Mother Ann had assured him there would be no cause to accuse them while they were aboard his ship. However, it quickly became clear that their opinions about what was due cause differed completely.

Right after the ship set sail, the Shakers "went forth and praised God in songs and dances." As James Whittaker later testified:

> This offended the Captain to such a degree, that he threatened to throw us overboard, if we attempted to go forth in this manner again.
>
> But Mother believed that it was better to hearken to God rather than man. So when we felt a gift of God, we went forth in the same manner, not fearing man, but trusting in God. This greatly enraged the Captain, and he attempted to put his threats into execution.

There then ensued another of the miracles which are one of the major ingredients of early Shaker history. Again in James Whittaker's words:

> But that God who had sent us had power to protect those that trusted in him; and this he did in a marvelous manner. It was in the time of a storm. The vessel sprung a leak, occasioned by the starting of a plank, and the water flowed in so rapidly that, though all the pumps were employed, the water gained upon us so fast that the Captain was greatly alarmed and turned as pale as a corpse.

27

But Mother maintained her confidence in God, and said, "Captain, be of good cheer, there shall not be a hair of our heads perish; we shall all arrive safe to America. I was just now sitting by the mast, and I saw a bright angel of God, through whom I received a promise." Soon after Mother had spoken the words, there came a great wave of the sea, and struck the vessel, and the plank suddenly closed to its place, and we were soon, in a great measure, released from the pumps.

Following this demonstration of Mother Ann's powers, "the Captain gave us freedom to worship God according to the dictates of our own consciences, and promised that he would never molest us again," the Whittaker testimony related. The remainder of the voyage was therefore uneventful, the ship arriving safely at New York on August 6, not quite three months after leaving England.

Having already put their full faith in the divine guidance of their leader, the small group of Shakers walked off the *Mariah* on a warm Sunday afternoon with no worries about how they would manage to establish themselves in this new land. On foot, they proceeded up Broad Way until Mother Ann felt a signal to turn into a side street. At a house where several residents were seated on the front steps enjoying the sunshine, Mother Ann stopped and spoke to them unhesitatingly.

"I am commissioned of the Almighty God," she said, "to preach the everlasting Gospel to America, and an Angel commanded me to come to this house, and to make a home for me and my people."

Whatever the emotions were that this remarkable statement provoked, the family so addressed did open their door to the travelers. At least a temporary refuge was provided until they could secure some kind of employment. Of necessity, though, they soon had to scatter, with Mother Ann herself remaining to work as a housemaid for their first American benefactors. Because she had always been accustomed to toiling for her bread, she had no sense of demeaning herself by doing menial labor, but another consideration made her long to leave the city household where she was kept busy scrubbing and polishing.

Her mission was to spread the message she had received in the Manchester prison, and even while awaiting more divine signs telling her how to start her ministry, she craved the comfort of being able to worship with her English followers. Toward this end, it seemed essential that they all gather together in their own quarters. But the worldliness she never lost despite her mystic leanings made her see clearly that they would need much money before they could acquire any property.

A trying winter elapsed while the members of the little group sought to earn enough for the next phase of their mission. For Mother Ann, the winter was particularly difficult because both illness and a personal crisis prevented her remaining with the family who had befriended her. The crisis, and perhaps the illness, too, rose out of the sudden relapse into sinful behavior of the man who persisted in thinking of himself as her husband.

Apparently Abraham Standerin swept aside the Shaker restraint he had seemed to accept and demanded that his wife live with him as a proper wife should. When she fiercely refused to do as he wished, he started drinking large quantities of rum and even took up with a woman of the streets. Mother Ann's suffering from the experience of

29

having to banish him forever from her sight made her unable to continue working. Living alone in an unheated room, she became seriously ill.

However, her friends would not let her lose hope. From some Quakers they had encountered, they heard about an area more than a hundred miles north of the city where land might be secured cheaply. John Hocknell, James Whittaker, and Mother Ann's brother William journeyed up the Hudson River to investigate. Although the tract proved to be mostly swampy wilderness, they thought it might be made to suit their purposes, so they arranged for a long-term lease.

It took them nearly another year to clear a portion of the land and build a simple log shelter there. Mother Ann spent the summer and winter of 1775 waiting in New York, but the Shaker annals give no evidence about how she existed during these fateful months for Britain's American colonies. Nor does the Shakers' own history make the slightest reference to the shots that had been fired at Lexington and Concord in April. The unfolding drama of the American struggle for independence seemingly had little impact on these recent arrivals from the Old World.

Mother Ann finally moved from New York City in the spring of 1776, which was a time of great excitement for New York residents. After the British forces left Boston in March, General George Washington thought New York would surely be the redcoats' next target, so he brought his own army there. The threat of impending fighting made many New Yorkers look for safety elsewhere. But few of the fleeing refugees could have chosen a haven as remote as Mother Ann's.

The land on which the Shaker men had settled was only

The Shakers in Niskayuna enjoying a sleigh ride THE NEW
YORK PUBLIC LIBRARY PICTURE COLLECTION

about seven miles northwest of Albany, but it had such a number of low and swampy spots that other people had spurned it in favor of higher and healthier locations. Comparatively close as they were to an old trading center, the Shakers were nonetheless almost cut off from civilization by wet marsh and forest. Yet the name the Indians had given the area, before being driven away by the early Dutch explorers, gave reason for hoping good crops might be raised here.

Niskayuna, the old Indian name for the area, meant "maize land." So even though the Shaker men lacked any real farming experience, they felt sure they could grow the food they needed once they cleared trees and brush and drained the ground water by digging ditches to divert it from their fields. All that was required was hard work, they thought, and they were willing to work as hard as necessary. In addition, because they each had some skill like blacksmithing, they expected to be able to earn part of their support by practicing their own trades in Albany during the winter.

Indeed they were following one of Mother Ann's favorite precepts: "Put your hands to work and your hearts to God," she had constantly told them. So when she arrived at their wilderness retreat and found them doing just as she had taught, she could only be pleased. Although the shelter they had constructed was merely a rough cabin, with a room at ground level for "the sisters" and a sort of attic space for "the brethren," she made no complaint about the primitive arrangements.

Instead she set herself to expanding the spiritual boundaries of her little community, for she had no doubt that soon new converts by the score would start coming to

Niskayuna, and she wanted to be ready to receive them. Her vision in the Manchester prison had confirmed her own belief that the basic sin besetting mankind was the lust that led to sexual relations between men and women. She had also been assured that any who gave up such sinful connection could be eternally saved and live as though in paradise, even while they still remained on earth. Nor was salvation impossible for those who had sinned in the past— if they would only confess their old sins freely and fully, then constantly struggle against being tempted to sin again.

These two principles of celibacy and confession already formed the foundation of the Shaker creed. Now, as Mother Ann labored in the wilderness to build a more complete religion, she was granted new visions which allowed her to see other aspects of the perfect life. She learned that the holding of any sort of personal property was incompatible with the perfection she was bent on achieving for her followers. So, too, all fighting and all wars were evil. And so was man's traditional assertion of superiority over women. Only the divine commands of God, as relayed through messages to His true believers, could set the rules for any individual's conduct

The more Mother Ann discovered during her frequent visions at Niskayuna, the more her followers became convinced that she was no ordinary mortal. From the French prophets who had first inspired them, the Shakers had accepted the belief that the second coming of Jesus Christ was imminent. Even before moving to the wilderness, they had begun feeling that the time of great happiness mentioned in the Bible—the millennium, when Christ would reappear on earth—might already have started. Now they became increasingly certain this was so.

For in the eyes of these devout worshippers, Mother Ann now seemed nothing less than the bodily rebirth of the same divinity that had first appeared as Christ. In the words of one of her followers: "The ultimate fruit of the labor and suffering of soul that Ann passed through was to purify and fitly prepare her for becoming a temple in whom the same Christ Spirit that had made a *first* appearing to Jesus . . . could make a *second* appearing."

So the small band of Shakers living at Niskayuna with Mother Ann felt lifted far above the worldly hardships they had to face, and they never thought to fret about enduring hunger or cold or other human privations. But after several years had passed, while they slowly tamed their wilderness, a different complaint arose among them. Why had no miraculous message spread the news of Mother Ann's arrival here? Where were all the poor sinners they were now prepared to receive?

Be patient, Mother Ann kept urging. In God's good time, the great work of gathering in converts would surely begin. And during the spring of 1780, at last the American pilgrims they had been expecting started to find them.

These first pilgrims had already been aroused to a high pitch of religious enthusiasm—and then been disappointed. Throughout the past several decades, there had been periods when a particular preacher had suddenly felt the call to renew the faith of his own flock by holding what had come to be known as revival meetings. Such revivals were supposed to bind wavering believers more closely into the fold of whatever church the newly inspired preacher represented. However, sometimes the religious emotion set free by these meetings in many of New England's small towns was left unsatisfied when the revival ended. The doctrines of conventional religion seemed too tame in the aftermath of the special excitement that had been generated. This kind of disillusion had followed an unusually fervent revival along the western border of Massachusetts and in the adjacent New York village of New Lebanon during the summer of 1779.

Throughout the next winter, some of the participants in these meetings had been despairing because salvation had, after all, eluded them. In March, two men decided a change of scene might ease their disappointment, and seemingly just happened to pass by Niskayuna. There the Shakers not only welcomed them warmly as if their appearance had been anticipated but also began explaining the Shaker faith.

Told that there was no need to wait any longer for Christ's second coming, and that anybody who accepted Shakerism could immediately be saved forever, the travelers were astounded. Instead of proceeding westward as they had planned, they hurried back home to report their remarkable discovery.

The man they reported to was a Baptist preacher named Joseph Meacham, who had been one of the leading figures in the recent revival. Besides being a fiery speaker, the thirty-eight-year-old Meacham was already widely known for the depth of his religious feeling. But though he was still searching for a stronger assurance of salvation than the so-called New Light Baptists seemed to offer, he was not ready to trust the claims made on behalf of Shakerism without inquiring more fully into their beliefs. He especially wanted an answer to a question that must disturb any careful reader of the Bible: How could it be possible that a female should lead the new religion?

Unless this unnatural situation could be satisfactorily

explained, Meacham saw no point in going himself to Niskayuna, so he sent one of his most reliable friends with
instructions to put a specific query to Mother Ann. Accordingly, as soon as Calvin Harlow reached the Shaker
community, he asked to be led into her presence, and he
solemnly stated:

"Saint Paul says, Let your women keep silence in the
Churches; for it is not permitted unto them to speak; but
they are commanded to be under obedience, as also saith the
law. And if they learn any thing, let them ask their husbands at home: for it is a shame for a woman to speak in
the Church. But you not only speak, but seem to be an
Elder in your Church. How do you reconcile this with the
Apostle's doctrine?"

As related in the Shaker annals, Mother Ann answered:

The order of man, in the natural creation, is a figure
of the order of God in the spiritual creation. As the order
of nature requires a man and a woman to produce offspring; so, where they both stand in the proper order,
the man is the first, and the woman the second in the
government of the family; He is the father and she the
Mother; and all the children, both male and female, must
be subject to their parents; and the woman, being second,
must be subject to her husband, who is the first; but when
the man is gone, the right of government belongs to the
woman: So is the family of Christ.

This reply apparently satisfied Joseph Meacham when
it was relayed to him, for within a few weeks he himself
led a group of New Light Baptists to Niskayuna. There
they were welcomed calmly by Mother Ann and her followers from England. Having foretold the coming of the
visitors, Mother Ann had seen to it that a meal was ready
when they arrived; then after the Americans and the Man-

chester immigrants had eaten together they settled down to a serious religious discussion.

Perhaps to avoid needlessly provoking distrust among the Americans, who might still be uncomfortable listening to a female expound religious gospel, Mother Ann had appointed James Whittaker as her spokesman. So the loyal James once more had an opportunity for proving his own exceptional powers. Ten years younger than Joseph Meacham, and lacking formal schooling or experience as a leader, he replied unhesitatingly to the older man's first question.

Why, Meacham demanded, did the Shakers here at Niskayuna feel it necessary to conduct the peculiar worship services he had heard described, and in general to follow such a strange way of life?

James said they had been laboring for many years to find redemption from sin and already had received many signs that their path was the only true road to salvation.

Meacham then asked about the Shaker visions, and he challenged every reply with some conflicting statement from the Bible. Unflustered through a whole long day of detailed questioning, James Whittaker patiently presented the Shaker point of view. Time after time he insisted that the Shakers had already proved it was possible for any person to achieve a perfect freedom from sin if he or she sincerely wished to do so and could thereby gain eternal bliss even while still remaining outwardly in mortal form.

At last, Meacham posed the crucial challenge. "Are *you* perfect?" he asked. "Do *you* live without sin?"

James Whittaker had his answer ready. "The Power of God, revealed in this day, does enable souls to cease from sin," he said, "and we have received that power; we have actually left off committing sin, and we live in daily obedience to the will of God."

Joseph Meacham had no more questions. "If you have attained to that which we have not, we should be glad to share with you," he said, "for we want to find the best way to be saved."

Thus a New England preacher voiced his newfound faith in the doctrines of Mother Ann, and from that day onward her first American convert tirelessly helped to spread her message.

Four

Persecutions

By July 1780, several dozen of the farm and village folk who had been stirred during the New Lebanon revival of the previous year had decided they must visit Niskayuna. The testimony of Joseph Meacham and Calvin Harlow made them feel a great desire to see Mother Ann themselves. While some were merely curious, others already felt disposed to look favorably upon Shakerism; but another sort of reaction was also increasingly noted.

Distrust, fear, and outright hatred—these were now being encountered more and more often by the Shakers. They not only found themselves facing persecution because of their religious beliefs but they had to contend with gossip that they were probably British spies.

For the American Revolution, which had seemed to make so little impression on Mother Ann and her followers, was still being fought. Although the main focus of the war had shifted away from New York, there still were occasional British raids along the Hudson River, and anyone who might support the redcoats was regarded with deep suspicion by upstate patriots.

As soon as the Shakers at Niskayuna began to attract attention, some people in the Albany area suspected them of being British sympathizers. After all, had they not come from the enemy country comparatively recently? Then, when the trickle of Niskayuna-bound travelers became a stream, the rumor that these Tories in the woods were dangerous spread for miles around. A flock of sheep brought the brewing trouble to a head.

The sheep were being driven to Niskayuna by a prosperous farmer from New Lebanon who wanted to do his part toward helping the Shakers feed their growing number of guests. But a group of Albany patriots thought there must be a more sinister reason why these sheep were being delivered to the secluded Shaker retreat. Could it be that these Tories somehow planned to provide a feast of mutton for British forces stationed along the lower reaches of the Hudson? Convinced of the logic of this supposition, the patriots hauled the New Lebanon farmer before a city magistrate on the charge of treason.

Mother Ann sent Joseph Meacham and John Hocknell to Albany to defend the unlucky farmer. As a result, all three were clapped into prison to await trial. But not satisfied that the real culprits were behind bars, the magistrate ordered an officer to arrest "the grand actress" at Niskayuna, and also several of her principal advisors. Thus, in short order, Mother Ann and her most devoted followers were all being held at Albany's old fort while local authorities debated how to deal with them.

One of those imprisoned was a recent convert who had formerly been a Presbyterian minister in New Lebanon. Accustomed to preaching, this Samuel Johnson boldly gave his captors a sermon on the subject of the evil of all war.

"People cannot follow Christ and live in wars and fighting," he insisted. To the Albany patriots, the teaching of such a doctrine at a time when the country was in great danger from an enemy army presented clear evidence of treason. There seemed no doubt, too, that Mother Ann was the main conspirator. While the other Shakers were held in Albany, it was decided to send her down to Poughkeepsie, where higher authorities might want to hand her over to the redcoats in exchange for some important patriot prisoner.

The Albany commission that ordered her removed southward inadvertently did her a favor. The jail to which she was taken in Poughkeepsie offered more opportunity for attracting public notice than could have been the case in the barricaded fort where she had originally been detained. From her Poughkeepsie cell, Mother Ann could—and did —cry out to passersby. And some who heard her soon spread word that a poor woman was being cruelly oppressed just because of her religious beliefs.

Then fair-minded citizens insisted on her transfer to a private dwelling. Although she was technically still a prisoner, she was allowed to receive visitors. Taking advantage of the sympathy her plight had aroused, Mother Ann began seeking new converts among her callers. She even conducted Shaker worship services, with a powerful show of singing and stamping, while she remained officially under a charge of treason.

That was too much for certain elements in the town. Whatever else this woman might be guilty of, they decided, she must surely be an emissary of the devil. So they organized their own protest, somewhat along the lines of the Boston Tea Party. Disguised with Indian-style paint and feathers, they surrounded the house where she was being kept and attempted to throw little bags of gunpowder through the windows into the fireplace.

When some of Mother Ann's friends were able to foil these efforts to blow up the building, the "Indians" secured a ladder and dropped a bag of powder down the chimney. But the divine aid that had already protected the Shaker leader on many past occasions again preserved her from injury, and the explosive bounced harmlessly away from the hearth.

Thereafter, according to the Shakers' own history, Mother Ann suffered no further harassment, although she was still held in Poughkeepsie against her will. Meanwhile, the wave of hysteria that had led Albany's local authorities to lock up the other Shakers gradually subsided. The men detained in the old fort were, one by one, set free—in the cases of the American-born, partly because their relatives gave affidavits that the Shaker converts were harmless lunatics, and in all of the cases because no shred of real evidence pointing toward treason could be uncovered.

When James Whittaker won his freedom, it was he who finally managed to bring Mother Ann's continued confinement to the personal notice of New York's Governor Clinton. Since at that time state business was being conducted from various mid-Hudson towns, nobody yet having proposed making Albany the capital, the Governor was doubtless speaking only the truth when he told Whittaker this was his first knowledge of the matter. For he immediately ordered that Mother Ann be granted her full liberty.

Thus after five months Mother Ann was able to return to Niskayuna. While she had endured no severe mistreatment, the fact that she had unjustly been kept in custody for so long was a blot on the record of the new state government, as the Governor's prompt pardon clearly admitted. Nevertheless, the experience provided her with an unexpected benefit.

Despite her best efforts during her imprisonment, Mother Ann had moved only two new converts to join the Shaker ranks while she remained in Poughkeepsie. But once she resumed her preaching amid her own followers, it quickly became apparent that her ordeal had accomplished more than she had imagined. Somehow the story was spreading that a remarkable woman had just been released from prison—a woman whose sole crime had been to espouse a strange new religion. In the sparsely settled farm country of New England and upper New York, religion was always likely to kindle a sudden emotional fire. The result was that potential converts by the score were soon descending on the Shaker retreat.

Instead of Niskayuna, the neighborhood was now more frequently called Watervliet even though the old Dutch village of that name was about five miles eastward. The Shakers themselves began to speak of their settlement as Watervliet around this time, possibly because in their minds Niskayuna was the wilderness where they had first entered upon their American adventure and their home no longer seemed so isolated. By now, a frame building had been constructed to serve as a combined dwelling and meetinghouse. Whenever the weather was sufficiently open to permit travel, another new group of visitors might be expected to appear.

The program awaiting the visitors might vary in some details, but generally each guest received an intensely personal appeal from Mother Ann herself or from one of her chief assistants. This process was known as "laboring,"

A schoolroom scene at the Niskayuna community THE NEW
YORK PUBLIC LIBRARY PICTURE COLLECTION

that is, bringing a new sinner into the spiritual state where confession of all past sins would pour forth. Then participation in the ecstatic Shaker worship could seem a glorious form of release. To the dispassionate observer, these services might have a fantastic quality rather like an exercise in mass hypnosis, and strong-minded disbelievers might describe the proceedings even less charitably, as a Baptist minister from Pittsfield, Massachusets, did in this account:

> When they meet together for their worship, they fall a-groaning and trembling, and every one acts alone for himself; one will fall prostrate on the floor, another on his knees and his head in his hands. . . . Some will be singing, each one his own tune; some without words, in an Indian tune, some sing jig tunes, some tunes of their own making, in an unknown mutter, which they call new tongues; some will be dancing, and others stand laughing, heartily and loudly; others will be drumming on the floor with their feet, as though a pair of drum-sticks were beating a ruff on a drum-head; others will be agonizing, as though they were in great pain; others jumping up and down; others fluttering over somebody, and talking to them; others will be shooing and hissing evil spirits out of the house, till the different tunes, groaning, jumping, dancing, drumming, laughing, talking and fluttering, shooing and hissing, makes a perfect bedlam; this they call the worship of God.

However, to the Shakers and their sympathizers, all this seemingly aimless uproar had a deeply religious significance. The more excited the worshippers became, the closer they felt toward achieving the utter peace of knowing themselves purged of every sin. And while some of the visitors invited to join in the sacred rites felt so repelled by what they saw and heard that they rejected any possibility of finding personal salvation through Shakerism, there were others who astounded even themselves by suddenly falling under the Shaker spell.

Indeed the contagion was such that Mother Ann rejoiced over her coming at last into the full possession of her divine powers. But with the practical streak that still distinguished her, she decided that she could reach many more souls if she herself would travel from village to village, instead of waiting until sinners should be drawn to her. So, in the spring of 1781, she set out on horseback, accompanied by her brother William, James Whittaker, and three others.

Their first stop was just a one-day journey, to a small settlement near the Massachusetts border. A few of the families here had already become believers during a visit to Watervliet, and they had promised to hold meetings in their own homes, providing Mother Ann with an opportunity for preaching to all those men and women from miles around who might consider embracing Shakerism. But other people disposed to distrust or fear any new religious ideas would not allow the meetings to proceed peacefully. One local minister even led his flock to try to break up a Shaker gathering on the Sabbath.

Then James Whittaker, now known as Elder James among the Shakers, stepped forward. "He advised the mob to let them alone," the Shaker history relates, "so that no acts of violence were committed."

Yet, when the Shaker party moved down into Connecticut, they had more trouble. No sooner had they arrived at the home of one of Joseph Meacham's brothers than a committee appeared to demand their immediate departure. No "witchcraft" would be tolerated in this place, the Shakers were told. Still, according to the testimony later collected by believers, the Shakers were not molested, despite many angry mutterings, when they dared to hold a meeting there.

However, the opposition mounted to such an extent at their next stop that Elder James suffered physical abuse. When he tried to reason with a mob threatening the Shakers in the Massachusetts village of Harvard, a volley of stones raised painful welts all over his body. In other towns, he was beaten with whips, or he and the other Shaker men had their eyes blackened, or were knocked down and trampled on the ground. Finally, Mother Ann herself was attacked brutally:

> They immediately seized her by her feet, and inhumanly dragged her, feet foremost, out of the house, and threw her into a sleigh, with as little ceremony as they would the dead carcase of a beast, and drove off, committing at the same time, acts of inhumanity and indecency which even savages would be ashamed of.

Rather than give up, though, the Shakers kept right on holding their meetings wherever they could assemble a few potential converts. Almost as if they thrived on their persecutions, they labored day and night to win new adherents, and the fervor of their efforts did attract at least a handful of believers practically every place they stopped. But their hardest work was concentrated in eight or ten communities where they were able to find enough willing listeners to lay the foundations for separate Shaker colonies. So it was with a sense of great reward that they finally returned to Watervliet after two years and four months on the road.

Yet as happy as their friends were to welcome them home, the Watervliet Shakers were also alarmed by the changes they could not help observing in their leaders. Mother Ann's brother William was four years younger than she, but his sturdy frame seemed shrunken by the trials he had suffered. Although no particular disease or injury afflicted him, his bodily strength was so diminished that he could hardly work any more, and even Mother Ann was failing.

It was September when the travelers came back from their journey, and through the whole of the following winter William kept growing weaker. Even the arrival of spring did not make him feel any better. In May 1784, when he was just forty-four years old, Mother Ann's brother died.

Then her own weakness increased so that her loving followers became deeply concerned. Mother Ann did all she could to keep them from grieving and to make them understand that she wished them to carry on her work after her departure. "I shall soon be taken out of this body," she told them, "but the gospel will never be taken away from you, if you are faithful."

Nevertheless, the few remaining Shakers who had come with her from England and the others who had learned to love her since her arrival in America could not help fearing what the future might bring. If Mother Ann left them, how would Shakerism survive? Was it not all too likely that the creed she had taught them would disappear with her?

Mother Ann herself assured them they had no cause to worry. "Be not discouraged, nor cast down," she urged them, "for God will not leave his people without a leader."

Still, the whole Shaker community at Watervliet was cast into gloom when Mother Ann spoke her last words to them. "I see brother William coming in a glorious chariot to take me home," she said on September 8, 1784. And then she closed her eyes.

Mother Ann was forty-eight years old when she died,

almost exactly ten years after she had crossed the ocean to establish a new religion in the New World. By the force of her own convictions she had gathered hundreds of followers, some of them thoughtful men and women with a sincere commitment to her religious principles. But there were others whose devotion had been stirred by Mother Ann herself, and at least some of these seemed to feel no further allegiance to Shakerism now that she could no longer lead them. So her death inevitably raised the basic question of how the religion she had founded could possibly be kept alive.

✣ *Five* ✣

Two Fathers

IMMEDIATELY AFTER MOTHER ANN'S FUNERAL, James Whittaker was moved to step forward, and he begged all of his brothers and sisters to pray for him. He needed their help to follow the path of God now that the most capable guide among them had departed, he told them with such emotional force nobody present could doubt the meaning of his words. Three days later, he was formally installed as the new leader of the Shakers.

Father James, they called him. Although he was then only thirty-three years old, men and women nearly twice his age accepted his right to the title. Since his boyhood, he had obviously had such a special relationship with Mother Ann that he did indeed seem like her spiritual son. And for her sake, he had willingly abandoned his own natural mother and father.

In the eyes of the Shakers, his intense religious zeal was seen as a sign of outstanding merit, but to nonbelievers his complete dedication might be regarded in a somewhat different light. By trade a weaver, he came from a family that had advanced beyond Toad Lane to the extent that they gave him a little basic schooling before he began his apprenticeship. So James Whittaker could sit down and write a letter to his parents if he wanted to.

It was they who had first taken him to religious meetings at the Wardleys' where Ann Lee was a fellow worshipper, but after she had seen her vision in prison and become the group's leader, the senior Whittakers could not accept her teaching. The young James had not only rejected their example but had pained them still further by joining the American expedition. Within a year of his arrival in the New World, they sent him word that they were both in failing health and appealed to him to come back to England. His reply bluntly told them:

> I hate your fleshly lives . . . as I hate the smoke of the bottomless pit. . . . Stay in England till you go down into your graves. . . . Away with your looking towards me for help. . . .

The same severity marked Father James when he rose to preach Mother Ann's doctrines. "Marriage of the flesh is an agreement with hell," he would shout. But his most bitter scorn was saved for any person who after embracing Shakerism gave up the faith and returned to worldly ways. Tree limbs would fall upon their heads, disease would strike them down, and the worst tortures of everlasting damnation would afflict them when they died, he would promise.

Despite the cold scorn Father James could show to disbelievers, among Shakers his mildness and loving kindness were said to be truly remarkable. So was his tireless energy. Only a few weeks after assuming the ministry, he set into motion a major new project.

He decreed that the first Shaker building to be used

exclusively for worship should rise on a site that an American follower agreed to make available. The donor was the same prosperous farmer whose sheep had led to the jailing of Mother Ann four years earlier. Now, instead of merely giving away part of his herd, David Darrow gave up his whole farm of several hundred acres. Because this rolling land outside the New York hamlet of New Lebanon was much more fertile than the Watervliet tract, Father James thought it made good sense to transfer the central authority of Shakerism there, about thirty miles to the southeast.

Not that Watervliet, with its holy memories as Mother Ann's first home in America, was to be left to return to the wilderness it had been when they had known it as Niska-yuna. Although its marshy forest had not yet been transformed into fruitful fields, and during some seasons the Shakers there had barely enough harvest to keep from starving, a colony would continue to work and pray at this sacred place. Another group of Shakers would create a second colony on the former Darrow farm. Being blessed with greater natural advantages, New Lebanon would, however, become the religion's main base of operations.

Father James now felt sure that the time had arrived when the next stage of Mother Ann's own program could be undertaken. She herself had clearly seen that unless Shakers withdrew from the world and lived in separate communities safe from outside interference, they could not practice their religion as they had visualized it. Family ties, in particular, would constantly upset true Shaker serenity. However, there had been no practical way of gathering all the early converts into private havens because the necessary land and buildings were much beyond their limited resources. The situation had changed, though, during recent years.

As a result of Mother Ann's missionary trip, there were clusters of well-off Shaker believers in at least half a dozen rural New England areas. It seemed to Father James that these people could be brought to feel the importance of pooling their property. Then, if others could be encouraged to join them, it was possible that Shaker villages might soon spring up all over the country.

Father James had no doubt that this glorious prospect would become reality if only he worked hard enough, so he flung all his energy into trying to organize new settlements. Without any thought about conserving his own strength, he traveled as far as New Hampshire during his first year as the Shakers' leader. When he returned to New Lebanon to bless the new meetinghouse in January 1786, he was elated by being able to report much progress.

However, his followers could easily note the price all this effort had cost him. At their urging, he promised to rest for several months at the Connecticut home of one of Joseph Meacham's brothers. But Father James could not remain idle, and he kept interrupting his rest with more traveling, until even he accepted the fact that he could not expect to see the achievement of his dream. Returning once more to New Lebanon, he told his dear friends that he felt his own work was almost finished. "I do not know that I shall ever see you again in this world," he said, "but I leave you with those who are able to teach you the way of God."

Then Father James went back once more to rest at the home of Joseph Meacham's brother, where he died a few months later on July 21, 1787.

So, after only three years, the Shakers again were left without a leader, but again there could hardly be any question about who would take up the task. Mother Ann herself had called Joseph Meacham her first-born American son, and she had predicted that he would one day "be a Father to all his people in America." Father James had showed his acceptance of this prophecy by gradually assigning some of his own duties to Mother Ann's American favorite.

Thus it was Father Joseph who now assumed the mission of carrying on the Shaker work. But if his elevation was no surprise, the skill with which he took over his new responsibilities made a lasting impression. Most historians agree that without the timely contributions of Joseph Meacham, Shakerism probably would have faded into insignificance before the start of the 1800's.

The first American-born Shaker leader was a tall, solemn man of forty-five when he took command of Mother Ann's faithful band. Religious laboring came natural to him because he had been brought up in an Enfield, Connecticut, household where Jonathan Edwards had exerted a profound influence. The great New England revivalist had delivered one of his most famous sermons in Enfield, inspiring Joseph's father to found the town's first Baptist church. By the age of sixteen, Joseph had impressed a neighbor as a "very intelligent" youth who "delighted much in conversation on religious subjects & on philosophy . . . but was not addicted to light frothy conversation." Even without any formal training in theology, for country people in those days did not demand to see a diploma before listening to a minister, Joseph Meacham was a respected Baptist preacher in the New Lebanon area when his search for a better way to assure eternal salvation led him to Niskayuna.

During the seven years he had already spent helping spread the Shaker gospel, he had apparently developed some definite ideas about the direction Shakerism ought to take. For there was a shrewd Yankee side to him, too, and under other circumstances he might have become a successful businessman. This became obvious from his swift and effective approach to the building program his predecessor had started.

In effect, he worked out standardized plans for the specific kinds of structures a Shaker community would require—the living quarters, the workshops, and, of course, the meetinghouses. Not that he sat down and made actual drawings, because basic principles were far more important to him than any abstract notions about beauty or balance. He just described the uses each type of building would have to be put to and insisted that the sturdiest but simplest methods of construction should be employed; and then he left matters of detail to the Shaker carpenters and other artisans assigned the task of carrying out his orders.

Father Joseph's general approach did not differ much from James Whittaker's, in the sense that the meetinghouses that rose under his direction were quite similar to the large plain structure Father James had built at New Lebanon. However, Father Joseph was able to accomplish incomparably more. During the first few years of his administration, he built eleven whole villages—at Watervliet and New Lebanon (later Mount Lebanon) in New York; Harvard, Hancock, Tyringham, and Shirley in Massachusetts; Enfield, Connecticut; Canterbury and Enfield,

New Hampshire; and Alfred and New Gloucester (later called Sabbathday Lake) in Maine.

Despite the magnitude of this achievement, however, the scope of Father Joseph's activities was much broader than mere buildings can indicate. He also created an entirely new pattern for communal living, complete with a carefully planned economic scheme to make the Shakers self-supporting, and a code of rules covering every aspect of personal behavior to promote the Shakers' spiritual well-being.

Because of his sincere conviction that Mother Ann had been divinely inspired, he made her own words into guiding maxims. "You ought to dress yourself in modest apparel," she had told a woman convert. "Every faithful man will go forth and plow his ground in season, and put his crops into the ground in season," she had often said, "and such a man may with confidence look for a blessing." Father Joseph quoted Mother Ann constantly, and he also started collecting the testimony about her life and works that was gradually written down over the next several decades in books comprising the Shaker equivalent of the Bible. But he was far more than just a loyal disciple.

Ever since Father Joseph's time, non-Shakers have tried to trace the origin of one or another of his ideas. There are scholars who say that the Shaker experiment was modeled on the primitive communism of some groups mentioned in the Bible, as well as on some nearly forgotten radical religious communities that cropped up during the Middle Ages. Professors who see the Industrial Revolution as the single most important influence on the modern world focus on Ann Lee's upbringing in Manchester, where children as young as four years old were hired to work fourteen hours a day under dreadful conditions. Shakerism, accord-

The Wash Shop of the North Family at Mount Lebanon LEES
STUDIOS PHOTOGRAPHERS   THE SHAKER MUSEUM, OLD
CHATHAM, NEW YORK

ing to these experts, was clearly a protest against the brutal inhumanity of the factory system.

But it is also possible to explain Shakerism in purely American terms. For its religious extremism resembles similar movements that have erupted onto the American scene from colonial times right up until the present. The Shaker emphasis on a simple rural life style as the ideal defense against worldly evil could appeal equally to Thomas Jefferson and readers of the *Whole Earth Catalog*. And notwithstanding the traditional American respect for rugged individualism, all sorts of communal enterprises have attracted supporters throughout the nation's history.

There are many sources from which Joseph Meacham may have gathered inspiration, and yet he probably deserves far more credit as an innovator than he is usually given. Certainly he had help in setting the Shakers on the path that a handful still follow. One of his first actions was to choose Lucy Wright to serve with him as the Shaker leader "in the female line." As she later demonstrated, she was an exceptionally able executive. Ann Lee's divine revelations provided the religious foundation upon which Shakerism would always be based, but it was Father Joseph who put together the framework for a unique form of community living.

How should a Shaker village be governed? What kinds of work should the residents do? What were the best ways for avoiding all worldly temptations? And how could frictions with the outer world be minimized? Questions like these challenged Father Joseph constantly, and within a single decade he arrived at his own answers to them.

During almost precisely this same period, the new United States adopted its Constitution and chose George

Washington as President to put it into effect. The Shakers had no such document setting forth the powers and responsibilities of their leaders. While there were many other differences between the positions of George Washington and of Joseph Meacham, the basic one had to do with this lack of any law to limit—or help—the Shaker leader.

So Father Joseph had to improvise a new kind of family structure for his followers even before he solved the larger problems raised by the Shaker separation from the rest of the world. As it happened, though, the living arrangement he developed turned out to be the most important single factor in making Shakerism workable, economically as well as religiously. For the family unit he established contained about sixty adults, with approximately the same number of brothers and sisters. Although there might be several families residing in the same village, each had its own supervising elders, its own dwelling, and its own fields and shops.

From the viewpoint of maintaining discipline, it seemed wise to him to keep each Shaker family comparatively small. Yet in the interests of preventing needless duplication of domestic duties like cooking, it seemed sensible to have the Shaker family substantially bigger than the typical worldly household. Happily for the whole future of Shakerism, Father Joseph's new variety of family also proved just about the right size to provide a highly effective working force in a simple agricultural economy.

Despite Shakerism's philosophy about female equality, Father Joseph found what he considered practical reasons to set definite lines of demarcation between men's work and women's work. Following worldly custom, he decreed that women should take charge of all housekeeping and of some other specific chores like making clothing, while men did the farming, blacksmithing, and furniture making. The same Shaker principles that dictated separate dwelling wings and dining tables and even separate doorways for each family's sisters and brothers also required separation of the sexes during working hours, Father Joseph believed. Nevertheless, because certain farm operations like gathering in the hay needed as many hands as could be mustered, he allowed temporary suspensions of the ordinary rules. Thus each Shaker family had specialized workers for every necessary task, and it also had the flexibility of being able to concentrate its whole working force on a particular job at peak periods.

Among political scientists, much is made of the fact that the early Shakers were actually practicing pure communism, no matter if they had never even heard the word. For each family's property was jointly owned, each worker carried out assigned tasks without regard to personal preference, and each individual was rewarded only by the sense of having contributed selflessly to the common good. Since food, clothing, shelter, and other needs such as nursing care were all freely available to family members, there appeared to be no necessity for paying any wages.

However, even if Father Joseph's Shaker families seem to fit the classic definition of communism, the broader picture shows various Shaker peculiarities. Owing to Shakerism's strict prohibition against any fleshly relationships, the most notable was its attitude toward children. Because no Shakers could become parents without sacrificing the basic tenet of their religion, outsiders constantly accused them of being fanatics bent on killing off the whole human race. The Shakers themselves always denied this, though, making use of all sorts of complicated theological language which, in essence, admitted something they refused to admit openly—that the majority of humankind would never embrace Shakerism.

Yet they could not explain away the plain truth that Shaker families were no different from other families in that they needed children to ensure the continuation of their line beyond a single generation. So Father Joseph had to give serious attention to several aspects of this particular problem.

Although many of the converts Shakerism attracted were already married and brought children into the fold with them, individual mothers or fathers could not be permitted to exert any influence on their own offspring. Mother Ann's teaching specifically warned against allowing personal feelings to interfere with Shaker love for all humanity. Therefore, children had to be separated from their parents, just as husbands and wives had to be kept from the danger of preserving prior attachments by being assigned to separate families. But Father Joseph thought that one Shaker family might safely be charged with raising the children of other dedicated Shakers.

Since a new generation of recruits would eventually have to be secured elsewhere, he also assigned each family the duty of giving a good Shaker upbringing to as many orphans as possible. Though detailed arrangements for special children's quarters did not evolve until somewhat later, Father Joseph established the Shakers' basic policy regarding children. Unlike many other communist experiments, Shakerism outlawed the last vestige of the traditional family from the time the first Shakers began living in what they called "gospel order." For parents were completely detached from their own children. But unlike various other monastic groups, which could rely on fellow believers who were not sworn to celibacy to provide a regular supply of new members, the Shakers always included the rearing of potential recruits among their responsibilities.

Indeed this was probably the most easily understandable difference between the Shakers and the religious societies fostered by some Roman Catholic orders of monks and nuns. There were, of course, other important differences in outlook and religious dogma, but many outsiders either could not or would not take the trouble to distinguish what these might be. At a time when anti-Catholic prejudice prevailed widely among rural and mainly Protestant Americans, anything smacking of "popery" was immediately and deeply suspect.

Still, the bigots who condemned Shakerism because of its surface resemblance to Roman Catholicism were, unknowingly, stating a case that did have some legitimate standing. For the governing code that Father Joseph developed for his flock bore more than a slight similarity to the ruling principles of the Church of Rome. Every Shaker was expected to accept the concept that all authority flowed from a single anointed leader, down through a chain of loyal bishops to the lowliest individual believer.

"A notable feature of their system," an unprejudiced observer wrote some years later, "is that the members do not appoint their rulers, nor are they consulted openly or directly about such appointments. The ministry are self-perpetuating; and they select and appoint all subordinates, being morally, but it seems not otherwise, responsible to the members."

In the case of Shakerism, however, the authority claimed by Father Joseph extended far beyond the sphere usually conceded to a religious leader—embracing such minute points of personal behavior as proper table manners. All Shakers in good standing were forbidden even to play with a cat or dog. In every imaginable area of daily living, and not merely in their religious conduct, Shakers were supposed to obey their leaders without question. To Father Joseph, such complete obedience was totally justifiable because the Shaker religion and the Shaker way of life could not be divided into separate categories. Living the perfect life *was* the Shaker religion. Therefore, no true Shaker could object to the loving guidance of any elder.

Although Father Joseph originated this grand Shaker design, and labored mightily during his nine years of leadership to evolve its countless details, he never put his rules into written form. So no outsider could claim to know what his exact words were, except those he used on the only official Shaker document surviving from his time in command.

This was a contract he drafted in 1795, setting forth the conditions under which converts were accepted into the Shaker faith. Because the relatives of some new Shakers objected strongly when the family property was donated to the religious community, Father Joseph thought a written agreement testifying that the gift had been made voluntarily would forestall trouble with worldly lawsuits. This covenant, which all subsequent recruits were required to sign, largely accomplished its aim of avoiding court cases. But it did not end Shakerism's difficulties with the outer world because there still remained one fertile source of anti-Shaker propaganda that no Shaker leader could silence.

Father Joseph had surely tried to avoid opening the Shaker ranks to anybody who would question the religion's principles. In the contract he drafted, he specified that no young person could be received as an actual member until reaching legal age. But despite all such efforts to keep out potential skeptics, a certain number of converts did find the Shaker life much less than perfect, and when they left the fold they were likely to talk bitterly about the experience.

The sole weapon the Shakers had against attacks by disillusioned converts was to call them liars—and every backslider during Shakerism's early years faced this charge. Since at least some of the backsliders were unstable, the testimony of this entire category of witnesses has sometimes been discounted by Shaker sympathizers, even in the present day.

Nevertheless, several women whose husbands attempted to lead their whole families into Shaker villages told similar stories. Neither malice nor coincidence can adequately explain the nearly identical accounts of early Shakerism provided by men and women who lived in different Shaker villages at different times within the same few decades. Most of their evidence pertains most directly to the period after Father Joseph's death in 1796 and during Mother Lucy's continued rule until her death in 1821, but much of what these witnesses said harks back to the basic pattern Father Joseph created. By an irony no convinced Shaker could ever appreciate, practically the only specific details about early Shaker life that have been preserved in print were set down by Shaker enemies.

Six

The Story of Eunice

IN THE YEAR 1802, a merchant named Hawley removed his family from Connecticut and took up storekeeping in the New York State hamlet of Durham. There his daughter Eunice met and soon married her father's respected young competitor, James Chapman. The couple had three children during the next several years. Eunice Chapman had no complaint about her husband.

"He treated me kindly until about the year 1809, when he visited the Shakers," she testified.

The testimony was offered before a committee of the New York State legislature during one of the most extraordinary legal squabbles of the early nineteenth century. In 1816, a time when a woman who married automatically lost the right to own property, to start a lawsuit, or even to keep her children if for any reason she and her husband were separated, Eunice Chapman had the audacity to demand help from the state's lawmakers after her husband took their three children with him into a Shaker community. No less a personage than former President Jefferson angrily commented that it would be "the darkest bigotry and barbarism" to heed this mother's request.

For if a man were to be deprived of his children merely because he chose to adopt the Shaker religion, would it not be a clear case of interference with the nation's cherished freedom of religion?

Many lawyers of high standing fully supported the Jeffersonian viewpoint, among them New York's attorney general, the politically ambitious young Martin Van Buren. It seemed quite safe to disregard any claim the mother in this case might have, since public opinion generally approved of the prevailing legal inferiority of women. Considering that only husbands and fathers were able to express their views at the polls, members of the legislature might have been expected to ignore or to ridicule Eunice Chapman's appeal.

However, unlike most of the other women whose lives were affected by Shakerism, and despite her own seemingly rural background, Eunice Chapman had a good grasp of political realities. She also had several powerful male relatives. Her father had by now become a postmaster, one of her brothers superintended the customs house in Rochester, and she had a brother-in-law serving as an alderman in the state's capital city, Albany. They knew her whole story, right from the beginning.

James Chapman, after first encountering the Shakers at Watervliet during a business trip, had gradually grown to feel that his own destiny lay with them. He spent longer and longer periods visiting Watervliet, but his behavior when he returned home hardly encouraged his wife to do as he wished and join him in seeking salvation there.

"He would force the children from the table and say, 'They shan't eat with such a sinner,' " she later recalled. "He often spit in my face, in their presence, and said it was the filthiest place he could find" because it was so defiled with sin.

Nevertheless, she finally did join him at Watervliet after he told her the Shakers there would provide a separate house for her and her children. However, immediately upon their arrival, the children were snatched from her and she was put in charge of Eldress Hannah, who informed her she was being accepted only on a trial basis. "She said I must confess my sins to her, and if I wished to see my children I must ask her liberty."

During the ensuing weeks, Eunice Chapman had many trying experiences:

> On January 5, I visited a family who were not Shakers. When I returned, I found they were displeased. They soon began their worship . . . spitting on their hands, stamping, and whirling about, and saying, "Hiss, hiss, hiss, hate the devil, hate the devil, chain the devil, chain the devil!" I opened the door because the noise so confused me, and my eyes were so filled with dust, that I was forced to retreat. The house shook so that I ran out of doors for safety. Surely, thought I, God can never be truly worshipped in such a manner.

> Next day, Hannah said I might think strange of their having such a meeting the evening before, but they were obliged to have such a meeting because I had been among the people of the world, and brought such a host of evil spirits, that they creeped all over them and even got into their mouths. I inquired if she could see them. She replied, "Yes." And how did they look? "They looked like caterpillars." Then she continued, "We always have such a meeting after the world's people have been among

us, in order to drive off their evil spirits, and chain them down, then we enjoy such peace as the world knows not of."

Although Eunice constantly asked to see her daughters and her son, whose ages then ranged from five to ten, Eldress Hannah kept finding excuses for denying the request. "Oh, Eunice, what a sinner you are!" the eldress continually told her. "What mercies you abuse for slighting the offers of salvation held out to you."

Indeed the only occupation she was permitted was to sit while Eldress Hannah labored for her conversion. "Oh, Eunice!" the eldress finally exclaimed. "In a very short time, you will lift up your eyes in torment, and behold me afar off, and you will call upon me to dip the tip of my finger in water to cool your parched tongue."

Eunice asked whether the eldress would give her the water.

"Nay," she said. "I shall not be permitted to do it. I shall sit in heaven and laugh!"

"What, Hannah, you will sit in heaven and laugh at my misery?"

"Yea, me and all the saints of God here—we shall laugh at your calamity and mock when your fear cometh."

That chilling exchange brought Eunice to realize she could not possibly accept Shakerism, and during a brief moment when she saw her husband, she told him so. However, she offered to let their children remain at Watervliet with him if only she were allowed to live quietly nearby and see them often. He replied that he could make no such arrangement without permission from Elder Calvin, and the next day the two men came to see her.

"I made some remark upon Mr. Chapman's obligation to

71

his family," Eunice Chapman testified later, "and upon my unhappy condition. I told my husband I was willing to stay there if it would be less expense to him, but could not embrace their religion, neither would I molest them in theirs.

"They said, 'Unless you unite with us, you cannot endure to live with such a pure and holy people . . .' They appeared anxious for me to depart. Hannah then took me by the arm and said, 'You must obey your husband,' and shoved me down stairs, held me till the other women put on my coat and hat in a ridiculous manner, shoved me out of the doors, and thrust me into an open wagon."

Then her husband and another Shaker drove her off to Albany, where they unceremoniously deposited her on a street corner. However, James Chapman and the other Shakers failed to reckon on the solidarity—and the influence —of the Hawley family. For the next several months, they were all busy talking to members of the state's legislature. As a result, a hearing was held by a committee of that body in March 1816, its first purpose being to discover the present whereabouts of the Chapman children, who had disappeared. Toward that end it had summoned one of the Shakers' senior elders, Seth Wells.

"Where is Mr. Chapman?" Elder Seth was asked. "And where are the children?"

"I cannot say."

"How did Mr. Chapman and the children go away?"

"I cannot say."

"How could Mr. Chapman take the children, and go from your house, without your knowing it?"

"I cannot say."

However, despite the steadfast Shaker refusal to concede any involvement, and despite the reluctance of many lawmakers to set what they considered might be a dangerous precedent, a majority of both houses of the legislature finally adopted a law "for the relief of Eunice Chapman."

Besides dissolving her marriage, the new law provided that any husband or wife whose spouse had joined the Shakers might take court action to secure the custody of his or her children. So Eunice Chapman won her battle, but her victory was less than complete.

After several more months of effort, she finally found her children at the New Hampshire Shaker village where they had been hidden. However, they treated her like a stranger when she appeared with a sheriff's deputy to enforce the court order she had obtained following the granting of her divorce. "How do you do, Eunice?" they inquired coldly. Faced by the obvious fact that they had been taught to hate her, she left the two girls, after all, and brought only her son back to New York with her.

How many other cases were there like Eunice Chapman's? A handful did come to light in various states, but they did not arouse any notable amount of public sympathy, for two reasons. Since Shakerism was most appealing to poor and uneducated country people, the wives who stood the best chance of being put in the same position were the least able to cope with the complications of securing a fair hearing. And those women who did fiercely insist on being heard almost of necessity had to use such a shrill tone that they could easily be dismissed as hysterical females. Typical of the latter was New Hampshire-born Mary Dyer, probably the widest known of the Shaker critics.

In its basic outlines, Mary Dyer's experience was quite similar to Eunice Chapman's, but her reaction was far more violent. Instead of merely attempting to solve her personal problem, Mrs. Dyer became so infuriated that she devoted much of the rest of her life to a campaign aimed at discrediting the Shakers. She sought out every former Shaker she could discover and assembled scores of affidavits allegedly proving that even Mother Ann herself had been immoral, a drunkard, and motivated only by greed.

Because the Dyer charges were so venomous, the Shakers were able to turn them to their own advantage. They published a number of books and pamphlets by devout Shakers, defending Mother Ann with what appeared to be unanswerable logic:

> Can any man or woman of common sense suppose that thousands of rational beings, born in a land of liberty and civilization, and brought up in the midst of moral and religious principles and instructions . . . would deny themselves of all worldly pleasures and enjoyments, and subject themselves to the dictates of a woman of base character, who lived in direct opposition to those principles which she daily preached to others?

The result was that the Shakers gained rather than lost by the spreading of spiteful attacks like Mary Dyer's. And the increasingly prosperous appearance of their villages added to the growing feeling among worldly people that Shakerism was more to be admired than condemned. As Mary Dyer herself admitted, the Shaker habits of industry and economy—"the strict order and regularity with which they proceed in their temporal affairs, the neatness and simplicity . . . of their establishments"—all tended to attract public esteem. Nevertheless, there were other witnesses more reliable than Mrs. Dyer who made the point that outer serenity might be just a surface covering for inner turmoil.

❦ *Seven* ❦

And Doubting Thomas

NOBODY COULD ACCUSE THOMAS BROWN of being subject
to hysteria. He was an exceedingly earnest Methodist
making his living as a traveling salesman in 1798 when he
came upon a pamphlet about the Shakers. Written by a
backslider, it described Shakerism unfavorably but stressed
the point that believers insisted theirs was the only true road
toward salvation. Thomas Brown, who had done a goodly
amount of religious reading, felt sufficient curiosity to decide he would investigate Shakerism himself.

Accordingly, he stopped at the Shaker village of Watervliet a few months later.

"I have come to see you," he told the elder who greeted
him, "to have a little conversation, if agreeable, concerning
your faith and religious profession, as I sincerely desire to
know your way of life and salvation."

The elder replied without hesitating. "To those who come
sincerely to inquire of us respecting our faith," he said, "we
are willing, according to our ability, to give all the information they desire."

Thus began a series of conversations the recounting of

which filled more than three hundred pages when Thomas Brown, ten years later, set down the whole story of his personal experience in a book entitled, *An Account of the People Called Shakers.*

The writer's desire to provide a fair picture is reflected on almost every page. Instead of merely stating that the Shakers obeyed Mother Ann's precepts about sharing with the less fortunate, he listed the contributions three Shaker villages sent when the needy of New York City were short of food during a yellow-fever epidemic: "300 dollars in specie, 853 lb. of pork, 1,951 lb. of beef, 1,794 lb. of mutton . . . and 26 dollars and 50 cents intended for the payment of freighting the articles from Hudson to New York."

However, the total impression of Thomas Brown's literary effort was quite the opposite of giving aid and comfort to Shakerism. He sent a copy of his manuscript to Mother Lucy Wright before having it printed, explaining, "I feel not, and therefore write not as an enemy; but merely give an impartial statement according to the best of my ability. . . . If it can be clearly pointed out to me, wherein I have not given a correct account, I shall be willing to alter and correct, as it is only my intention to act the part of a faithful historian." Replying on Mother Lucy's behalf, one of her aides scornfully dismissed the work as not being worth reading because "We know thee, Thomas; and be thy opinion whatever it may concerning thy own abilities, we must candidly tell thee that we are far from considering thee competent to the task thou has undertaken. . . ." It is easy to understand why the Shakers would wish to discredit this doubting Thomas, for his detailed account of Shakerism behind the scenes is probably the most damaging document ever written about the personal cost of trying to live the perfect life.

Thomas Brown's deep concern about eternal salvation disposed him to look favorably on Shakerism at first. During his initial visit at Watervliet, the answers to his specific questions concerning Shaker religious beliefs all satisfied him. And his own serious outlook apparently made a favorable impression on the Shaker elder assigned to labor with him. So Elder Benjamin "invited me to stay two or three weeks, and go among them and see for myself, till I was fully satisfied."

Thomas did spend several weeks living with other families at the village. Each was at a different stage of commitment to Shakerism, ranging from the most recent converts to those who had proved by their devotion that they were entitled to enter the inner circle reserved for the purest believers. During his stay, Thomas was on the whole pleased by what he saw and heard, but there were still a few reservations in his mind, as he informed Elder Benjamin.

"I told him, they held to some doctrines with which I could not fully unite. He said, 'That is of little consequence; we do not differ with one another because we cannot believe alike in every respect; neither shall we with you. And those things you cannot see into, leave them, and embrace or unite with what you do believe is right.' "

That struck Thomas as a reasonable attitude. "I considered of all I had heard and seen," he wrote later. "I thought assuredly I saw that order, peace, and union I never saw before. I felt a love toward the people for the love and kindness they manifested to me. I thought if they were what they professed to be, they were just such a Christian people as I long had wanted to find."

So Thomas confessed his past sins to Elder Benjamin, and thereby entered into the first stage of his close association with Shakerism. But although he already thought of himself as a Shaker, there were several reasons why he held back from taking the decisive step of coming to live in one of their villages. Among these were the fact that he had a wife and family, and while his memoir pays scant attention to such personal details, apparently he was unwilling to move from his home in the Hudson Valley village of Cornwall unless his family willingly went with him. Even after his wife and father did agree to become Shakers, Thomas still hesitated to give up his business and his home.

At least for a few years, Elder Benjamin and his Shaker superiors accepted Thomas's reluctance because it actually helped them. In Cornwall and along his travels, Thomas constantly preached Shakerism and brought a number of converts into the fold. So every time the subject of his entering a Shaker family was discussed, Thomas could point out how much he was accomplishing for the cause by remaining outside—and the truth of his argument could not be disputed.

Nevertheless, it also seemed clear that Thomas enjoyed the independence of his position. For his living apart let him avoid the constant subjection to Shaker discipline that was the lot of every family member. He cheerfully spent weeks at a time visiting Watervliet or New Lebanon or Hancock, but he still made excuses when he was asked to sign the Shaker compact formally signifying that he had united his person and his property with one or another of the Shaker communities.

It was the issue of dancing that finally ended the Shakers' patience with Thomas. One of his early questions about Shakerism had related to its religious exercises, which worldly people ridiculed as sacrilegious jigging done under the pretense of worshipping. Elder Benjamin had assured him, "Dancing is the gift of God to the church. . . . In this exercise we receive the strength and consolation to which the world are total strangers." From his own readings, Thomas knew that ancient religious sects had based their worship on dancing, so he accepted the Shaker explanation. As his own faith strengthened, he even felt the impulse to participate in the dancing himself.

"I began to have operations of shaking, trembling and stamping, similar to some of my brothers and sisters at Watervliet," he wrote, "and likewise a gift, as it is called, of speaking languages, or unknown tongues. The things I did I did not do as a sham, nor with intentions to make others think I was under the influence of divine power; but I really and sincerely believed I was influenced by the power of God."

However, after Thomas began dancing as well as preaching during the meetings he held on his own, several Shaker elders visited his home. He was away at the time, but they "left orders for me not to labor, or dance," only to assemble with possible converts. The instructions distressed Thomas.

Once previously he had objected when a few elders had told him not to allow a friend of his to do any Shaker preaching. "I told the Elders I did not fully agree with them," he wrote. "They made me no reply, but only told me to be *obedient*. This was the first time I heard of obedience to the Elders."

Yet once having heard the word, Thomas hesitated to argue about the matter of his dancing. Instead he thought about why he might have been asked to cease dancing. "On a little consideration, I saw the reason, which was . . . their belief that their dancing for worship is so sacred, reverential and awfully solemn, that no person dare, or can join in it, who has not confessed his sins." And non-Shakers attending his meetings had indeed been tempted to join him in dancing.

Still the manner in which the elders had made known their displeasure could not help irking Thomas. Why had they not explained, or requested, instead of "ordering" him to obey them? As Thomas thought back over his experiences with the Shakers during the past few years, he saw a pattern he had failed to note before. "Now I began to conclude that the Elders stood as sole leaders, teachers, and directors," he wrote "and that acquiescence and obedience to them was what in all things was required."

The realization deeply troubled him—to the extent that for the next several years he kept debating with his Shaker friends and wavering within his own mind. He still craved the salvation Shakerism promised. But how could he accept the complete sacrifice of his personal freedom that Shakerism apparently required? The larger part of his book charts the struggle he went through as he kept making new and disquieting discoveries:

> As soon as I could get a convenient opportunity to converse with the Elders, I inquired of them the reason and propriety of Elder E. Cooley's breaking open a letter

A sacred dance of the Shakers at Mount Lebanon, at a time when the dances had become somewhat ritualized WORCESTER ART MUSEUM, WORCESTER, MASSACHUSETTS

I had sent to a young believer. They said but very little as an apology; but afterwards I found it was the order of the church, and practice of the Elders, to intercept and break open all letters sent to any of the believers; principally to see if they contain any thing contrary to the faith.

Then a woman Thomas had led to become a Shaker angrily told him she was leaving the faith. "I am not going to be led by popes," she said. Her anger had been stirred by receiving a lecture from an eldress informing her that obedience to the ministry was the basic doctrine of Shakerism.

Still, Thomas tried to believe the elders had not deceived him. He listened patiently while Benjamin explained that salvation could not be expected all at once, immediately upon confessing past sins, but must be striven for laboriously and achieved only gradually. In this long process, the help of elders who had already passed through all the lower stages was indispensable. "Without the Elders," Thomas determined, "we are totally helpless, and can do nothing as to our salvation."

Accordingly, in 1802 he at last agreed to move his family from Cornwall. But he still could not give up complete control of his daily life to the elders, so he rented a house only a mile north of the Shaker village at Watervliet, close enough to permit him to worship frequently with his friends and still allow him some privacy. To ease the elders' displeasure at his holding back from complete surrender, he offered the valid excuse that he had some business debts which must be paid before he could sign their compact. On their part, they showed their feelings about his compromise arrangement by withdrawing their previous permission for him to preach Shakerism at any meeting.

Neither side would admit defeat. Thomas craved salvation as earnestly as ever, and the elders wanted this sinner to join their ranks because he had already proved himself a powerful religious speaker whose words could sway many other doubters. So the laboring over the soul of Thomas Brown continued for several more years.

"You teach, or counsel me, 'to renounce my business—to move to Watervliet—gather among the believers, and go to work, or be obedient to all things as you direct,'" Thomas told Elder Hezekiah, who had now assumed charge of his case. "I know what will follow, step after step—first I must put away all my books, and read no more, that I may learn nothing but what I learn from you. The next step, I must come into one of those families who have all things in common, my wife perhaps in one family, and I into another, and my children I know not where; and, it may be, I may seldom or never see her or them any more. . . . Therefore I think I had best 'look before I leap.'"

Thomas once pointed out that many sects down through the centuries had also advanced their own doctrine as the only sure way toward salvation. From his reading, he described the teachings of Emanuel Swedenborg, an eighteenth-century Swedish mystic, and of several French and English visionaries whose teachings ran counter to Shakerism. "There is a possibility of your being mistaken," Thomas noted.

Hezekiah had his answer ready. "Ah, Thomas must put away his books," he said, "if he intends to become a good believer."

For reading was no advantage to any Shaker, the elder explained, and that was why the children being brought up by the Shakers were usually given just a few lessons so they could read and write a little. "Even that they can do without," Hezekiah said. "To be obedient to what we are taught by our Elders, that is enough."

Then Thomas had to muse:

> So I must put away my books and leave off reading, and pattern after my brethren and sisters, to be in union; two-thirds of whom, from year to year (especially those in church order) don't take a book in their hands, not even the Scriptures. Though they have time to read, particularly in the winter, as they leave off work about sunset, wash themselves, and retire into their rooms; there they sit until nine or ten o'clock, except about a quarter of an hour at supper, and about the same time at family meeting—they arise at four o'clock in the morning, and soon assemble for worship—they breakfast about daylight, and do no work until near sunrise, in which time, morning and evening, they have at least five hours leisure—often nodding and sleeping. I have told them, I thought they had better spend their time in reading to one another some edifying books. "Nay, there is no gift for so doing"—they can do nothing without a gift. Keep in the gift, is all the cry.

By now Thomas could not help being aware that the Shaker elders were tired of debating with him. But some of his friends among the believers told him why Hezekiah and the others still continued their efforts. "It is easier to gain a thousand ignorant, unlearned persons, than one who is learned and well read," they explained. "But when such a one is gained, he is worth a thousand of the former." Although the implied compliment pleased him, he had his own reason for going on. "I mean to abide with them until I am fully convinced whether this is the only way of God or not," he wrote.

For despite the objections he kept raising, he had to

admit to himself that "there were many things I believed in common with them." He still felt that "the order, love and unity" of the Shakers exceeded that of any other people he knew. He appreciated the "meek, mild and quiet spirit" with which the elders bore his constant questions.

Nevertheless, in 1804 the Shaker leadership finally decided that having a doubter in their midst could no longer be tolerated. Thomas was ordered to make up his mind, once and for all, whether he would enter fully into a Shaker family. Then his soul-searching reached a feverish pitch.

Day after day, he walked the floor of the small room at Watervliet where he stayed during his ordeal. He took almost no food, he wept repeatedly when Elder Hezekiah told him he would never have another chance to embrace Shakerism if he gave up this last opportunity.

"I think it is likely," Hezekiah said at last, "that you will come to nothing, and be a poor creature, like many others who have turned their backs on the way of God. And you will not be able totally to lose your faith; the impression it has made on your mind will abide, and it will be your torment as it hath been to others, who have turned off—it will be your and their torment in hell! What a pity, when you might become a bright man in the gospel."

The threat stung Thomas to make a sarcastic answer. "I told him, it would be a droll story for me to tell the world that I was turned off, disowned, and all doors shut against me because I would not confess my sins the fourth time."

"Tell them the true cause," Hezekiah said. "That you would not take up your cross and be obedient to the order of God among his people—tell them this!"

Thomas replied: "Yes, I will tell them this, and more. For if I undertake to tell the world any thing about it I will not tell them half a story, but give them a true and full account of all matters that have transpired from first to last, and they may judge for themselves whether you are the people of God or not."

Yet Thomas did make one more attempt to suppress all his doubts, and he entered the Shaker ranks for the sake of his eternal salvation. However, within a few months, the obedience required of him had completely eroded his faith. He reached the point of doubting all the Shaker miracles, and he even decided that the Shaker dancing was caused by "imagination, zeal, enthusiastic fire, or rather religious madness, whereby the nerves which proceed from the brain to all parts of the body are affected."

In his new state of complete disbelief, he did write the book he had told Elder Hezekiah he might publish. With several similar works composed by other backsliders, it gave readers down through the decades a picture of Shakerism that exposed what lay beneath the peace and beauty of early Shaker villages. But books like these appealed mainly to people who put a high price on personal freedom, and many other people, either by choice or necessity, prized other values more highly.

The security of not having to worry about money was the greatest possible boon some people could imagine. Others sympathized with the feeling of the Shaker elders that the spiritual profit resulting from giving up all personal striving was worth the loss of individual liberty. Even thoughtful critics of the American system often posed the question of whether any venture in cooperative living could possibly succeed without a rigid religious framework such as Shakerism provided—and the more disturbed they were by various abuses of a free-enterprise economy, the less they were likely to be concerned about Shaker limits on personal behavior.

So the image of Shakerism, in the world outside and certainly among devout believers, did not suffer much from the negative voice of writers such as Thomas Brown. Indeed, it was during the years immediately following publication of Brown's volume that Shakerism enjoyed its greatest successes—not only in the East but now also in the West.

✤ *Eight* ✤

Opening the West

In 1799, accounts began appearing in Eastern newspapers about some astonishing religious meetings far away in the Western wilderness. Actually, thousands of ex-soldiers and others afflicted with wanderlust had been streaming beyond the Appalachian Mountains since the end of the Revolutionary War. While only muddy trails connected most of the isolated settlements these pioneers had founded, the advance of civilization through formerly untracked swamps and forest was already unmistakable.

With a population approaching 200,000, Kentucky had become a state in 1792. The Ohio territory could boast scarcely 50,000 settlers as the turn of the century approached, but it was growing so rapidly that statehood would be granted in 1803. Yet the hardships attending this great westward push seemed to breed a startling epidemic of religious agitation. In the words of one witness:

> On the edge of the prairie, multitudes came together and encamped on the ground for several days and nights.
> . . . There were present seven Presbyterian clergymen [who spoke] with tenderness and tears, that elicited the deepest emotions among the audience.

Their bodily agitations or exercises were various and called by various names, as the falling exercise—the jerks—the dancing exercise—the barking exercise—the laughing and singing exercise, etc. The falling exercise was very common. . . . The subject of this exercise would, generally with a piercing scream, fall like a log on the floor, earth, or mud, and appear as dead. . . .

The jerks cannot be so easily described. Sometimes the subject of the jerks would be affected in some one member of the body and sometimes in the whole system. When the head alone was affected it would be jerked backward and forward, or from side to side, so quickly that the features of the face could not be distinguished. When the whole system was affected, I have seen the person stand in one place, and jerk backward and forward in a quick succession, their heads nearly touching the floor behind and before. . . . Though so awful to behold, I do not remember that any one of the thousands I have seen ever sustained an injury in body. This was as strange as the exercise itself.

The dancing exercise. This generally began with the jerks. . . . Such dancing was indeed heavenly to the spectators; there was nothing in it like levity. . . . Sometimes the motion was quick, and sometimes slow. Thus they continued to move forward and backward in the same track or alley till nature seemed exhausted, and they would fall prostrate on the floor or earth, unless caught by those standing by.

The barking exercise (as opponents contemptuously called it) was nothing but the jerks. A person affected with the jerks, especially in the head, would often make a grunt, or bark, if you please, from the suddenness of the jerk. This name of barking seems to have its origin from an old Presbyterian preacher of East Tennessee. He had gone into the woods for private devotion, and was seized by the jerks. Standing near a sapling, he caught hold of it, to prevent his falling, and as his head jerked back, he uttered a grunt or kind of noise similar to a bark, his face being turned upwards. Some wag discovered him in this position, and reported that he found him barking up a tree.

The laughing exercise was frequent, confined solely with the religious. It was a loud, hearty laughter, but one *sui generis;* it excited laughter in none else. The subject appeared rapturously solemn, and his thoughts excited solemnity in saints and sinners. It is truly indescribable.

The running exercise was nothing more than, that persons feeling something of these bodily agitations, through fear, attempted to run away, and thus escape from them; but it commonly happened that they ran not far before they fell, or became so greatly agitated that they could proceed no further.

I shall close this chapter with the singing exercise. This is more unaccountable than anything else I ever saw. The subject in a very happy state of mind would sing most melodiously, not from the mouth or nose, but entirely in the breast, the sounds issuing thence. Such music silenced everything, and attracted the attention of all. It was most heavenly. None could ever be tired of hearing it.

Despite the Shakers' self-imposed separation from the outside world, the news about the remarkable religious awakening in the West gradually penetrated into their villages. It caused much discussion among the Shaker leadership, which had been concerned because the vast tide of new converts predicted by Mother Ann had not yet materialized. Converts were slowly increasing the size of the eleven existing communities in the Northeast, but sufficient recruits to justify the founding of additional villages were not being attracted. So the possibility that a fertile ground for their laboring might be found elsewhere engaged Mother Lucy's prayers until she received divine guidance about what she must do.

On New Year's Day, 1805, she sent three of her most trusted aides on a journey. They were charged with the mission of visiting the distant places where such a notable upsurge in religious feeling appeared to be in progress and if in their judgment the omens for a Shaker awakening seemed to be favorable, they were to bring Mother Ann's gospel to the West.

The three men she selected were all able preachers who had proved their devotion to Shakerism. Benjamin Youngs was the same Elder Benjamin who had first impressed Thomas Brown as such a convincing religious debater. John Meacham, the eldest son of the revered Father Joseph, had inherited an imposing physical presence as well as an exceptional talent for planning and organizing. Issachar Bates, the very model of a reformed sinner, had run off to fight at Bunker Hill when he was only seventeen, and being too young to bear arms had played the fife throughout the Revolution and practiced every sort of vice, before the Shaker message changed him into a tireless foe of evil.

These three set out on foot, with just one horse to carry their baggage. Unfazed by winter snow or mountain gales, they walked more than twelve hundred miles in two and a half months, arriving in the present neighborhood of Lexington, Kentucky, toward the middle of March. Here they found the first evidence of the religious revival they had come so far to investigate. Most importantly, they met a tall, gaunt Presbyterian minister named Richard Mc-Nemar.

A man of unusual learning for this time and place, McNemar could read Latin, Greek, and Hebrew easily.

Born in Pennsylvania in 1770, he had moved down through the mountains with his family during his boyhood. But besides becoming accustomed to surviving in the wilderness, he had also managed to acquire much more than the common allotment of schooling in the Ohio River village of Cincinnati. While still in his twenties, he had been licensed to preach by the governing body of the Presbyterian Church, and his congregation at Turtle Creek was one of the largest in the area.

Yet the doctrine he had been taught could not satisfy his yearning for some stronger assurance of salvation. Before he had ever heard of the Shakers, Richard McNemar was already leading revival meetings seeking a "new light" to guide sinners struggling to be saved. Because the established leadership of his church could not approve of such preaching, the New Light Presbyterians had recently broken away—and at least some of them were eagerly ready to welcome the Shaker missionaries.

The three soberly dressed travelers made their first Western convert only five days after their arrival at Turtle Creek. Malcolm Worley, a well-off farmer who had willingly taken the strangers into his home, proved equally willing to accept their religion. Then, once he had signified his faith in Shakerism by confessing his past sins, he brought his new mentors to visit the Reverend McNemar.

McNemar was living in a log cabin on his small farm, from which he tried to reap sufficient food for his large family. Besides his wife Jenny, a North Carolina woman, he had seven children, the youngest of them sorely afflicted. While still an infant, this boy, James, had crawled off alone. His mother found him near a black snake, its head raised to strike. With a shriek, she seized the child and ran into the house, fearing the snake was at her heels. Her fright was such that she nearly fainted. From that day onward, James had been subject to screaming fits, which had been growing gradually worse, and no treatment had been found that could help him. It happened that just as the Shaker group had begun laboring with Richard McNemar, James burst into the room screaming.

"If you will cure my child of this malady," McNemar said solemnly, "I will believe your doctrines."

The Shakers had made no claim of being able to work miracles, and none of the three was moved to speak. When their silence became uncomfortable, Jenny McNemar rose and said, "Let us pray." Not until the prayer ended did anybody notice that James was missing. He was discovered outside in the yard playing peacefully. Still, it could not be known till more time had elapsed that he would never have another attack.

A few days later Richard McNemar was walking through a meadow and saw the arm of a woman reaching down from heaven for him. He instantly recognized Mother Ann. "I will follow thee ever," he said. Thenceforth, he became the major figure in the second great expansion of Shakerism.

Not that he was able to bring the whole New Light movement into the Shaker fold. At the large camp meeting he arranged just a month after his own conversion, many of the thousands who gathered to hear the new prophets from the East angrily shouted down every Shaker sermon. "They are liars! They are liars!" other New Light ministers exclaimed. Their main objection to the gospel of Mother Ann lay in its basic theme that marriage must be condemned and that no married person could be saved. Such teaching was itself evil in that it contradicted the Bible's own words, some of the other New Light Presbyterians kept insisting. Intense excitement stirred the assembled group. Many people surrounded John Meacham, spitting at him and threatening tar and feathers. Others in the crowd howled suggestions to burn these false prophets. Still others, who must have been starved for entertainment on their remote farms, saw the whole performance as high comedy and laughed until they thought their sides would split.

Nevertheless, at smaller meetings in Malcolm Worley's home and in Richard McNemar's church, the Shaker cause scored notable gains. Elder Benjamin kept a diary recounting the travelers' experiences, and some of the entries tell of happier episodes from the Shaker viewpoint:

Jenny McNemar got exercised in dancing for some time. . . . Richard also got to dancing & Polly Kimball a woman of 27 who had not opened her mind was exercised . . . and from this she went to turning which was the first regular gift of turning we had seen since we left New Lebanon—& This she said she never had before, though she had both Jerks & dancing. . . .

A few weeks later:

Thence to Elijah's when in the evening several families of the believers met. . . . The meeting was 14 in all— we labored 4 or 5 songs & from thence exercises began which lasted full 4 hours—numbers were exercised in a sort of jerking, singing, dancing, turning in abundance, running round & about—the singing of Polly Kimball was Solemn and Singular.

But Polly Kimball was not the only convert:

> In the evening a few in number met to whom B[enjamin]
> and Jn [Meacham] spoke abt an hour—after this we spent
> 2 or 3 hours in singing—during which time several were
> remarkably exercised—particularly Sally Montford . . .
> her exercises continued near or quite 4 hours & were
> enough (if possible) to convert a nation. . . .

Although converting the whole population still did not
seem likely, since violent attacks on the Shakers continued
to break up some of their meetings, the number of believers
steadily increased. "We thank thee, O God," one of them
proclaimed, "that thou hast sent a chariot of fire from the
East, drawn by three white horses, to bring the everlasting
gospel to this land." Early in the summer of 1805, Mother
Lucy was so encouraged by the reports she received from
the West that she sent another three missionaries to help
in the good work.

The fruits of all this labor soon were visible. In 1806,
two Shaker villages were established in Ohio, and one in
Kentucky. The next year marked the formal gathering of
another Kentucky settlement, followed shortly afterward
by one in Indiana. Within the decade, two more Ohio
villages were founded, like the other Western communities
on land contributed by believers with large farms. They
were at some distance from any worldly town so that their
precise location is not easy to pinpoint on a modern map,
except in the case of the Ohio village whose site later became the Cleveland suburb of Shaker Heights. One of the
Kentucky centers was on Malcolm Worley's farm near
Lexington, the other in Logan County near the Tennessee
border; the other three Ohio villages were in Adams County
on the Ohio River, in Warren County northeast of Cin-

cinnati, and in Montgomery County southeast of Dayton. The Indiana village, which had to be abandoned after only a little more than a decade because malarial swampland made it so unhealthy, was near Busro Creek on the Wabash River.

Including the ill-fated Busro venture, the seven Shaker villages in the West gave the religion a new importance mere numbers cannot indicate. It was no longer just a local curiosity and suddenly appeared to merit a closer look. In the East and in the West, visiting a Shaker community— particularly on a Sunday, when the remarkable worship service could be observed—became a favorite outing for other Americans.

This new sightseeing fad was the most notable sign of a change in Shakerism itself, as well as in the prevailing attitude toward it. Around 1820, the fervor that had marked the first Shakers gave way to a different feeling. The faith of devout believers was no less intense, they were sure, but now they no longer had to depend on inspiration for their every move. They had experience to guide them, and during Mother Lucy's last years as their leader, she showed her understanding that another era would soon be starting by having certain songs written down. A regular order of worship was established for Sunday-morning services. And the policy of allowing, or even encouraging, strangers to attend was instituted.

Mother Lucy's purpose was clear. She hoped that at least some among the worldly people who came to stare would instead have their hearts touched and would be moved to join the Shakers. How often this happened nobody can say. For the Shakers kept no accurate membership statistics— probably with good reason. Despite the increasing attention they attracted, the actual numbers of converts they made could not have been very impressive.

According to the most reliable estimates, the Shaker villages in the West had about 2,700 residents during the late 1820's, and those in the East about 3,700. The latter figure includes a few hundred western New Yorkers who set up the colony of Groveland near Rochester in 1826. But even though the population of the nineteen Shaker villages was probably less than 6,500, in both the East and the West the Shakers had a much stronger impact on nineteenth-century America than such limited numbers would suggest.

Unhappily for Mother Lucy and her successors, the religious aspects of Shakerism stirred the least serious interest. It was the economic side of the Shaker experiment that really influenced outsiders, not only on Sundays, when they inspected thriving Shaker farms of surpassing neatness, but on every day of the week, when they purchased various Shaker products of superior quality at honest prices.

Right from the beginning, Father Joseph had realized that even the most independent community of Shakers would have difficulty surviving if its aim was to be completely self-sustaining. For there were bound to be certain tools or supplies the residents would not be able to produce for themselves, and unless the Shakers had some way of making money, they would not be able to buy this necessary equipment in the outside world. Most of the crops they could raise would be needed to feed their own members, so another sort of industry would have to be encouraged as a source of income.

Within just a few years, several likely ideas had been tried, and they proved admirably suited to the Shaker life style. By the early 1790's, Shaker gardeners in several communities had started to produce high-quality garden seeds, Shaker women were packaging the seeds in handy small packets, and Shaker peddlers driving horse-drawn carts were selling the seeds all over the surrounding countryside. Since the Shakers were among the first people to think of packaging seeds, they soon had a small but money-making business. Before their entry into this line of work, practically the only seeds for sale were distributed in barrels or large cloth bags from which smaller quantities had to be weighed out. As the difference in quality between the contents of the Shaker packets and the carelessly handled bulk supplies sold by storekeepers became known, the Shaker seed trade expanded. By the 1820's, SHAKER printed on a seed-package label was probably more familiar to Americans than any other meaning of the word.

Then some of the Shaker trustees who attended to all business with the outer world had a further thought. Printed booklets informing gardeners of the different kinds of vegetable, herb, and flower seeds the Shakers had available were soon being widely distributed. Eventually the booklets were expanded to include gardening directions. Instead of merely driving around their own areas delivering seeds, teams of trustees divided up much of the country and went on selling trips lasting several weeks or even months.

In the same general way, the Shakers also made their brooms and their chairs into household bywords. They grew a special variety of corn and from its stalks produced straw for long-lasting brooms shaped to sweep the narrowest corner clean. And their straight wooden chairs with woven seats were so sturdy yet lightweight and inexpen-

99

sive that many ordinary Americans came to depend upon them, despite their less obvious flaw of being comfortable only to people with extraordinarily straight backs.

Indeed these chairs could be considered a symbol of the popular impression of Shakerism toward the middle of the last century. Handsome to look at, but stiffly uncomfortable on closer acquaintance, the Shaker villages were admired by many outsiders, but few wanted to live in them.

There was, nevertheless, a category of Americans who increasingly found the Shakers' freedom from economic hardship worth the sacrifice of other worldly liberties. Women left widowed with young children, but without any means of supporting them, were discovering that they and their offspring could be saved from the miseries of the poorhouse by embracing this increasingly respected religion.

By the terms of the Shaker compact, revised in some details since Father Joseph's time but still in essence the same document, children could not be accepted formally as Shakers until they reached their legal majority. Friendless mothers seeking refuge with the Shakers were often willing to sign the compact themselves, being certain that their own future would thereby be assured and that their children would eventually be able to make their own choice. From the Shaker standpoint, the result was extremely disappointing. By the 1830's, they were becoming aware that only about one out of every ten children they raised was electing to remain with them upon attaining maturity.

How could they hold the younger generation? It is doubtful that any set plan was made for the special effort that began in 1837, first in the East and later in the West. After Mother Lucy's death in 1821, leadership of the New Lebanon ministry had fallen to elders who lacked any

Shaker seed box, lent to storekeepers for displaying and selling packets of seeds LEES STUDIOS PHOTOGRAPHERS THE SHAKER MUSEUM, OLD CHATHAM, NEW YORK

personal acquaintance with Mother Ann. Perhaps the realization that they required inspiration helped to account for the sudden flurry of messages their young followers started to receive.

The messages supposedly came supernaturally, sent by the spirits of Mother Ann and other departed Shaker leaders. Nevertheless, the elders and eldresses in charge of the families then living at Watervliet were more than willing to listen when they were told about the opening of this new line of communication one August afternoon. Girls between the ages of ten and fourteen, instead of dutifully sitting still while a sister gave them a lesson in religious dogma, had jumped up and stretched their arms toward unseen angels. After a remarkable display of whirling and singing, they had reported actually visiting heaven and hearing Mother Ann's own words. Although any ordinary lapse in discipline could be expected to provoke stern lecturing, in this case the reaction from the elders was so favorable that further visitations were eagerly awaited.

Not only at Watervliet but at all the other Shaker villages in the East and in the West, a new atmosphere of excitement stirred young and old alike. Under the circumstances, it was not long before other spirit communications were reported. When the anticipated manifestation reached Ohio, Elder James Prescott of the North Union colony was ready to record what happened:

> It was in the year 1838, in the latter part of the summer, some young sisters were walking together on the bank of the creek, not far from the hemlock grove, west of what is called the Mill Family, where they heard some beautiful singing, which seemed to be in the air just above their heads.

They were taken by surprise, listened with admiration, and then hastened home to report the phenomenon. Some of them afterwards were chosen mediums for the "spirits." We had been informed, by letter, that there was a marvelous work going on in some of the Eastern societies, particularly at New Lebanon, New York, and Watervliet, near Albany. And when it reached us in the West, we should all know it, and we did know it. . . .

It commenced among the little girls in the children's order, who were assembled in an upper room, the doors being shut, holding a meeting by themselves, when the invisibles began to make themselves known. It was on the Sabbath-day, while engaged in our usual exercises, that a messenger came and informed the elders in great haste that there was something uncommon going on in the girls' department. The elders brought our meeting to a close as soon as circumstances would admit, and went over to witness the singular and strange phenomenon.

When we entered the apartment, we saw that the girls were under the influence of a power not their own—they were hurried round the room, back and forth as swiftly as if driven by the wind—and no one could stop them. If any attempts were made in that direction, it was found impossible, showing conclusively that they were under a controlling influence that was irresistible. Suddenly they were prostrated upon the floor, apparently unconscious of what was going on around them. With their eyes closed, muscles strained, joints stiff, they were taken up and laid upon beds, mattresses, etc.

They then began holding converse with their guardian spirits and others, some of whom they once knew in the form, making graceful motions with their hands—talking audibly so that all in the room could hear and understand, and form some idea of their whereabouts in the spiritual realms they were exploring in the land of souls. This was only the beginning of a series of "spirit manifestations," the most remarkable we ever expected to witness on the earth. One prominent feature of these manifestations was the gift of songs, hymns, and anthems—new, heavenly, and melodious. The first inspired song we ever heard from the "spirit world," with words attached, was the following, sung by one of the young sisters, while in vision, with great power and demonstration of the spirit, called by the invisible

THE SONG OF A HERALD

Prepare, O ye faithful,
  To fight the good fight;
Sing, O ye redeemed,
  Who walk in the light.

Come low, O ye haughty,
  Come down and repent.
Disperse, O ye naughty,
  Who will not relent.

For Mother is coming—
  Oh, hear the glad sound—
To comfort her children
  Wherever they're found. . . .

From the girls' department to the boys', and then to the adult membership of every Shaker village, the receiving of spirit messages spread phenomenally for almost ten years. During this time, uncounted new songs were added to the Shaker hymn collections—and despite their supposedly heavenly origin, their quick and jiggy tempo something like the tunes black slaves were then singing would later strike some music students as an authentic American invention. The Shaker beat, it would even be said, had helped to lead to twentieth-century jazz.

Spirits also gave the Shakers another art form. Although

the painting of decorative pictures had previously been forbidden as a worldly vanity, pictures inspired by spirits were considered sacred. So dozens of spiritual paintings of subjects like "The Tree of Life" appeared on Shaker walls in the 1840's.

More frequently, though, the spirit messengers brought invisible spiritual presents, such as bowls of heavenly fruit far more delicious than any visible, earthly variety. Or they decreed new forms of worship, mainly open-air meetings at some particularly sanctified plot of ground. New spiritual names like Mount Sinai or Vale of Peace were given to these hallowed areas. Gradually, the regular work and worship schedule of the Shakers was suspended because spirit messages were arriving so often.

If the elders of every Shaker village had failed to encourage the reporting of such communications, surely the excitement would have evaporated in short order. However, the enthusiasm the spirits aroused gave Shakerism a new surge of energy so powerful that the leadership called the whole phenomenon "Mother Ann's Work." But apart from its immediate effects, the spiritualist upheaval had the added significance of indicating that the Shakers definitely belonged in the American mainstream. Within another few years, two young sisters from upstate New York who received messages from the other world via mysterious foot tappings would spread the spiritualist craze all across the country.

But this spiritual frenzy of the Shakers, expanding the mystic leanings upon which the religion rested, eventually reached a stage where it could no longer be tolerated. Even in the spirit world, apparently, evil had not been abolished. For spiteful messages began arriving, exposing some

One of the most attractive of the Shaker spirit drawings. The script underneath the drawing says: City of Peace Monday July 3rd, 1854. I received a draft of a beautiful Tree pencil'd on a large sheet of white paper bearing ripe fruit. I saw it plainly; it looked very singular and curious to me. I have since learned that this tree grows in the Spirit Land. Afterwards the spirit shew'd me plainly the branches, leaves and fruit, painted or drawn upon paper. The leaves were check'd or cross'd and the same colors you see here. I entreated Mother Ann to tell me the name of this tree; which she did Oct. 1st 4th hour P.M. by moving the hand of a medium to write twice over Your Tree is the Tree of Life. Seen and painted by, Hannah Cohoon SHAKER COMMUNITY, INC., PITTSFIELD, MASSACHU-SETTS

alleged sin committed by a Shaker child or even a Shaker elder, and demanding that the sinner be punished. When a girl in Kentucky received a spiritual communication accusing Richard McNemar himself of being unfit for Shaker leadership, the New Lebanon ministry finally decided there were false spirits as well as true spirits, and that henceforth special care must be taken to avoid being deceived by agents of the devil.

By that time, the excess of spirit-induced exuberance had brought a temporary halt to the reception of visitors at Shaker worship services. But within a few years, as "Mother Ann's Work" subsided, the communities again began welcoming outsiders.

Before and after the great spiritual excitement, dozens of observers both foreign and domestic had tried their hands at describing the Shaker devotions. Writers both anonymous and famous let their impressions be printed, and there is no better way of finding out how Shakerism toward the middle of the nineteeneth century struck the contemporary observer than to consult some of these old volumes.

Nine

Two Views

In 1832, a New York printer issued a short book with the following title page:

PECULIARITIES OF THE SHAKERS
Described in a Series of Letters
from Lebanon Springs

by a Visitor

This author has never been identified, but anonymous or not, he or she had a talent for composing clear and effective prose, as this opening passage shows:

> You have no doubt heard many strange stories respecting the worship and doctrines of this remarkable people, and it may appear singular that any reasonable person should ever be disposed to join them; for, if half the stories which have been circulated of them were true, you might justly conclude that they are fitter subjects for a lunatic asylum than to be intrusted with the affairs of a decent and well-regulated community. . . .

Nevertheless, the writer was sufficiently fair-minded to investigate personally the various rumors about the

Shakers, and toward that end went to their main center at New Lebanon in New York. The Shaker village there was only about two miles from Lebanon Springs, a summer resort for invalids and people of fashion. Originally, the mineral-rich water issuing from a picturesque outcropping of rock had been the principal attraction of the area because it was supposed to benefit skin disorders. But within recent years the nearby Shaker settlement had become an even greater magnet for large crowds, especially on Sundays:

The next day being Sunday, we repaired to their place of worship, which is one of the neatest buildings, both inside and out, that I have ever seen. The floor appears perfectly smooth, except a single seam in the middle of it, which seems to be the line of demarcation between the men and the women. On this floor there are moveable benches, which are brought in, both for the accommodation of visitors when the galleries are filled, as well as for themselves.

Here were assembled probably two hundred and fifty members of the Society, and about four hundred visitors, who were seated in and before the galleries, the men on one wing and the women on the other. Notwithstanding they pay every attention to their comfort, they shew but little taste in their dress, either males or females. The females, in particular, seem a shapeless mass of petticoat and handkerchief, surmounted by a large white Quaker cap, in no way calculated to improve their external appearance. They all look remarkably pale and sallow, and their countenances appear placid, there is not any striking evidence of happiness. The men generally looked healthy and ruddy, but the odd manner in which their hair is cut, as well as the antique form of their dress, gave them a very singular appearance. Among the number we noted several coloured persons, male and female, who were dressed in the same costume as the other members, and joined with them in their worship.

The worship commenced by the men arranging themselves in lines in one end of the room, and the women in the other, and after a few words were addressed to them by the Elder, they all kneeled down in opposite lines, facing each other, and after a period of profound silence, they commenced singing hymns from a book, the words of which were unintelligible to the auditors. After this they rose and marched backwards and forwards, facing each other, to a tune which they all sung; then they faced the wall, with their backs to the audience, and marched in the same manner, backwards and forwards towards the wall.

When this exercise ended they formed two circles, a smaller and larger one, and marched to the tunes sung by the inner circle, which composed the principal singers; their hands also keeping time, either by the alternate motion of swinging backwards and forwards, or by clapping them together as they became animated by the tunes which were sung. This exercise continued about half an hour, when they retired to their seats.

This observer went on to report that the New Lebanon Shaker village was handsomely situated in a valley surrounded by lofty, wooded hills. There were about fifty buildings, comprising the dwellings, barns, and workshops of the several families whose total membership amounted to between six and seven hundred persons. Their competence in harnessing the power of small streams to run the machinery of their workshops was notable, as was the orderliness of their extensive orchards and seed gardens. A store offering a variety of useful and well-made articles for sale attracted wide patronage, partly because of the Shaker reputation for producing durable goods at reasonable prices and partly because many of the guests desired a memento of their visit. In every respect, the Shakers treated their visitors hospitably.

The anonymous writer concluded:

You will probably ask my opinion of this remarkable Society. . . . In reply to which, I will very frankly declare that I think there is less mental anxiety and suffering, and more negative happiness among this people, than can be found in any other sect or community of the same number of persons. I say *negative happiness*, because the alpha and omega of their system of ethics consists in self denial. When they have arrived at that state in which they can deny themselves of all those intellectual and physical enjoyments which we consider indispensable to our happiness, their wants are extremely few, and these being amply provided for by the Society, they have no possible need of any anxiety whatever. They rise in the morning and perform their wonted labor, which is only sufficient to contribute toward their health; they partake of the plain and wholesome food which is set before them without desiring the delicacies or luxuries of the world; they clothe themselves with very plain, but clean and comfortable apparel, without any regard to the fluctuating rules which govern the fashionable portion of mankind; they pursue the even tenor of their way in the regular exercise of labor and devotion, regardless of the opinions and frowns of spectators, and thus continue, until, in a good old age, they fall asleep, and are buried with their fathers. Having no direct interest in the politics of the country, they give themselves no concern who is *in* office, or who is *out*, they mind their *own* business and leave all these matters to those who may feel an interest in them. A people acting under the influence of such principles, if they have not much positive enjoyment, cannot be exposed to much actual misery, because their condition precludes them from being subject to the same wants, anxieties and disappointments which afflict persons of other societies. They are exempted from the allurements, temptations, and trials which those have to contend with who are obliged to mix in the bustle of the world, and to come in contact with the artifices and intrigues of corrupt and deceitful men.

I can easily conceive that to persons who have been disappointed in their expectations and become disgusted with the world, to such as have a strong inclination to engage in extraordinary religious devotion, and to those also, who are not capable of taking care of themselves, this Society holds out strong inducements. It presents to them a resting place from the storms and buffetings of an angry world, an asylum of peace and tranquillity, a home for the helpless and wretched, where they may serve their Creator, and render themselves useful and comparatively happy. . . .

No one can say how many readers were attracted by this anonymous observer, but apparently the peculiarities of the Shakers was a popular topic. Magazine articles, pamphlets, and books gave the public a wide choice of literature on the subject. Even the most famous writer of the day, Charles Dickens, provided his own impressions of Shakerism.

By 1842, Dickens was a celebrity on both sides of the Atlantic, and his novels were eagerly read, chapter by chapter, as they appeared serially in popular booklets. When he arrived on his first visit to this country, he came prepared with pocket notebooks. For six months, he enthusiastically applied his powers of observation to every aspect of the American scene, from the museums of Boston to the riverboats plying the Mississippi.

Dickens found much to admire in the young United States, and he praised what he liked with great vigor in the *American Notes* he published on his return home to

England. But when he disliked what he saw, he expressed his feeling just as vigorously. Except for the hideous American habit of spitting tobacco juice in and around the ever-present American disgrace called the spittoon, nothing in his whole American experience depressed him as deeply as the visit he made just a few days before sailing home.

Having returned to New York City from the West five days before his ship was due to depart, Dickens took advantage of this unanticipated opportunity to visit a Shaker community.

I had a great desire to see "the Shaker Village," which is peopled by a religious sect from whom it takes its name. To this end, we went up the North River again, as far as the town of Hudson and there hired an extra to carry us to Lebanon, thirty miles distant. . . . The country through which the road meandered was rich and beautiful; the weather very fine; and for many miles the Kaatskill Mountains, where Rip Van Winkle and the ghostly Dutchmen played at ninepins one memorable gusty afternoon, towered in the blue distance, like stately clouds. At one point, as we ascended a steep hill, athwart whose base a railroad, yet constructing, took its course, we came upon an Irish colony. With means at hand of building decent cabins, it was wonderful to see how clumsy, rough, and wretched its hovels were. The best were poor protection from the weather; the worst let in the wind and rain through wide breaches in the roofs of sodden grass, and in the walls of mud; and were imperfectly propped up by stakes and poles; all were ruinous and filthy. Hideously ugly old women and very buxom young ones, pigs, dogs, men, children, babies, pots, kettles, dunghills, vile refuse, rank straw, and standing water, all wallowing together in an inseparable heap, composed the furniture of every dark and dirty hut.

Between nine and ten o'clock at night, we arrived at

115

Lebanon; which is renowned for its warm baths, and for a great hotel, well adapted, I have no doubt, to the gregarious tastes of those seekers after health or pleasure who repair here, but inexpressibly comfortless to me. We were shown into an immense apartment, lighted by two dim candles, called the drawing-room: from which there was a descent by a flight of steps to another vast desert, called the dining-room: our bedchambers were among certain long rows of little whitewashed cells, which opened from either side of a dreary passage; and were so like rooms in a prison that I half expected to be locked up when I went to bed, and listened involuntarily for the turning of the key on the outside. There need be baths somewhere in the neighborhood, for the other washing arrangements were on as limited scale as I ever saw, even in America: indeed, these bedrooms were so very bare of even such common luxuries as chairs, that I should say they were not provided with enough of anything, but that I bethink myself of our having been most bountifully bitten all night.

The house is very pleasantly situated, however, and we had a good breakfast. That done, we went to visit our place of destination, which was some two miles off, and the way to which was soon indicated by a finger-post, whereupon was painted, "To the Shaker Village."

As we rode along, we passed a party of Shakers, who were at work upon the road: who wore the broadest of all broad-brimmed hats; and were in all visible respects such very wooden men, that I felt about as much sympathy for them, and as much interest in them, as if they had been so many figureheads of ships. Presently we came to the beginning of the village, and alighting at the door of a house where the Shaker manufactures are sold, and which is the headquarters of the elders, requested permission to see the Shaker worship.

Pending the conveyance of this request to some person in authority, we walked into a grim room, where several

116

grim hats were hanging on grim pegs, and the time was grimly told by a grim clock, which uttered every tick with a kind of struggle, as if it broke the grim silence reluctantly, and under protest. Ranged against the wall were six or eight stiff high-backed chairs, and they partook so strongly of the general grimness, that one would much rather have sat on the floor than incurred the slightest obligation to any of them.

Presently, there stalked into this apartment, a grim old Shaker, with eyes as hard, and dull, and cold, as the great round metal buttons on his coat and waistcoat: a sort of calm goblin. Being informed of our desire, he produced a newspaper where a body of elders, whereof he was a member, had advertised but a few days before, that in consequence of certain unseemly interruptions which their worship had received from strangers, their chapel was closed to the public for the space of one year.

As nothing was to be urged in opposition to this reasonable arrangement, we requested leave to make some trifling purchases of Shaker goods; which was grimly conceded. We accordingly repaired to a store in the same house and on the opposite side of the passage, where the stock was presided over by something alive in a russet case, which the elder said was a woman; and which I suppose *was* a woman, though I should not have suspected it.

On the opposite side of the road was their place of worship; a cool clean edifice of wood, with large windows and green blinds like a spacious summer-house. As there was no getting in to this place, and nothing was to be done but walk up and down, and look at it and the other buildings in the village (which were chiefly of wood, painted a dark red like English barns, and composed of many stories, like English factories), I have nothing to communicate to the reader, beyond the scanty results I gleaned while our purchases were making.

These people are called Shakers from their peculiar

form of adoration, which consists of a dance, performed by the men and women of all ages, who arranged themselves for that purpose in opposite parties; the men first divesting themselves of their hats and coats, which they gravely hang against the wall before they begin; and tying a ribbon round their short-sleeves, as though they were going to be bled. They accompany themselves with a droning, humming noise, and dance until they are quite exhausted, alternately advancing and retiring in a preposterous sort of trot. The effect is said to be unspeakably absurd: and if I may judge from a print of this ceremony which I have in my possession, and which I am informed by those who have visited the chapel is perfectly accurate, it must be infinitely grotesque.

They are governed by a woman, and her rule is understood to be absolute, though she has the assistance of a council of elders. She lives, it is said, in strict seclusion, in certain rooms above the chapel, and is never shown to profane eyes. If she at all resembles the lady who presided over the store, it is a great charity to keep her as close as possible, and I cannot too strongly express my perfect concurrence with this benevolent proceeding.

All the possessions and revenues of the settlement are thrown into a common stock, which is managed by the elders. As they have made converts among people who were well to do in the world, and are frugal and thrifty, it is understood that this fund prospers: the more especially as they have made large purchases of land. Nor is this at Lebanon the only Shaker settlement: there are, I think, at least three others.

They are good farmers, and all their produce is eagerly purchased and highly esteemed. "Shaker seeds," "Shaker herbs," and "Shaker distilled waters" are commonly announced for sale in the shops of towns and cities. They are good breeders of cattle, and are kind and merciful to the brute creation. Consequently, Shaker beasts seldom fail to find a ready market.

They eat and drink together, after the Spartan model, at a great public table. There is no union of the sexes, and every Shaker, male and female, is devoted to a life of celibacy. Rumor has been busy upon this theme, but here again I must refer to the lady of the store, and say, that if many of the sister Shakers resemble her, I treat all such slander as bearing on its face the strongest marks of wild improbability. But that they take as proselytes, persons so young that they cannot know their own minds, and cannot possess much strength of resolution in this or any other respect, I can assert from my own observation of the extreme juvenality of certain youthful Shakers whom I saw at work among the party on the road.

They are said to be good drivers of bargains, but to be honest and just in their transactions, and even in horse-dealing to resist those thievish tendencies which would seem, for some undiscovered reason, to be almost inseparable from that branch of traffic. In all matters they hold their own course quietly, live in their gloomy silent commonwealth, and show little desire to interfere with other people.

This is well enough, but nevertheless I cannot, I confess, incline towards the Shakers; view them with much favor, or extend towards them any very lenient construction. I so abhor, and from my soul detest that bad spirit, no matter by what class or sect it may be entertained, which would strip life of its healthful graces, rob youth of its innocent pleasures, pluck from maturity and age their pleasant adornments, and make existence but a narrow path towards the grave. . . .

Dickens concluded his account by expressing "a hearty dislike of the old Shakers" and "a hearty pity for the young ones." Yet the picture was not quite as grim as it might be, he said, because of the strong probability that the "young ones" would run away when they grew older and wiser.

119

✣ *Ten* ✣

Prudence for the Defense

THE SHAKERS often had occasion to travel from one of their communities to another. In 1847, Sister Prudence Morrell, with Sister Eliza, Elder John, and Brother Lewis, left New Lebanon on a journey all the way to Kentucky, stopping at eight Shaker villages before returning home. Throughout the journey she kept a diary, and although she lacked the literary skill of a Dickens, she wrote, nevertheless, with an artless simplicity. During the four and a half months of her trip, from May through October, she recorded much of interest, and there remains no better defense of the Shaker cause than Sister Prudence's diary.

The four Shakers used every available means of transportation, from open wagon to stagecoach to railroad to riverboat. Of necessity they were sometimes housed in public hotels, and Sister Prudence could not help observing many strange aspects of worldly living. In her diary, she noted a few curious sights that give little dashes of the flavor of mid-nineteenth-century America, such as:

May 24th   The sun has arisen bright and the boat has quickened its pace. . . . About 2 o'clock we passed

Hanging Rock, about 150 miles above Cincinnati; there we saw a house where a man once lived that was pretty rich and feeling unwilling to have any enjoy his riches excepting his family he made his wife promise him before his death that she would never marry while he was above ground. So he prepared for himself an iron coffin and requested to be put into this iron coffin and placed back of his house above ground. And his wife had it set on two large pillars, a little frame built over it, and a large glass ball on top. There it remained fourteen years, and about one year ago the woman hired a man in the neighborhood to bury the coffin out of her sight underground which he did for one hundred dollars.

Or, while riding from one of the Kentucky Shaker villages to the other:

We have been traveling all day . . . but there is nothing scarcely to be seen on this road but stones and ruts, hills and hollows, ticks and jiggers, cabins and dogs, black children and hogs, horses and mules, slaves and slave holders, and the like. As for the road, it is too bad to talk about among decent people, and we had a tremendous shower in the bargain.

However, by far the largest portion of the diary is devoted to describing what the Shaker travelers found and what they felt at each of the Shaker villages they visited. Sister Prudence was fifty-three when she undertook the journey, and for the past several years she had been living at New Lebanon, but apparently she had first accepted the Shaker faith in Ohio. So her return to the West was in a sense a homecoming. Nevertheless, the joy she experienced upon reaching the haven of a Shaker community was repeated each time she entered any Shaker settlement, whether or not she had the mere earthly pleasure of encountering old friends there.

"We had a blessed good meeting at least it felt so to me," she wrote on one such occasion, "for I had been among the world so long that I felt needy of something to refresh my poor soul."

Indeed, the real value of the diary lies in its unstudied picture of Shakerism as seen from the viewpoint of a devout believer. The entry dated July 4 offers one of the best examples:

In the afternoon we attended church meeting. We had a good and precious feast of love and simplicity. The meeting began by bowing in thanks to God for the gospel and the blessings which we daily enjoy. After some exercises we sat down on the floor to gather simplicity. When we arose to our feet James McNemar spake of the vast difference there is between the sense of the world and that of Believers. The world, said he, was generally employed on the 4th of July to show how big they could appear, full of vanity and carousing, gaining no good to themselves nor doing any good to others; but we have been striving to see who can be the least, and I feel sure that we have received a beautiful store of good things by our simplicity and devotedness in the worship of God.

Or, in an entirely different vein, after arriving at the Kentucky Shaker village called Pleasant Hill, Sister Prudence wrote:

Aug 20th We are now at Pleasant Hill, feasting on good things. This we realize every time we stop anywhere among Believers, for when we are traveling among the world in this state we cannot get anything to eat but what is cooked by the colored people that look as dirty and greasy as an old saddle cloth, and a great deal of their victuals taste more like soap grease than anything fit for humans to eat. Traveling in Kentucky to see good Believers is some like climbing a thorn tree to get honey.

Despite her derogatory comments about the black cooks, Sister Prudence belonged to a society that not only opposed slavery but also admitted any black converts who wished to join their faith. What her personal feelings were can probably be gathered more accurately from another entry during her travels in slaveholding Kentucky:

> This morning we left South Union for Pleasant Hill at 5 o'clock. Cross'd Great Barrens and past Bowling Green. The colored people at work but the lazy whites sitting round thick enough to breed the plague. We met a slave holder this forenoon, he had 30 slaves. They were traveling to the South afoot about 25 miles a day. They were from Kentucky and Virginia. Their master gave 700 dollars for some of them, for some 600, others 500. We asked them what they had to eat? They said nothing but bacon & bread, coffee, twice a day. What does your master eat? He eats butter & bread and green tea and so on. . . .
> What a privilege, I enjoy a free salvation from sin surrounded by kind friends who furnish me with plenty to eat, drink, & wear.

But that Sister Prudence felt her religion offered far more than material comforts is clear to any reader of her diary. Her joy in the spiritual side of Shakerism shines forth on every page. "We went forth in the dances, and shook off all pride, lust, self-will, and everything that goes to hinder a free circulation of the pure spirit of Mother," she wrote after one of their prayer meetings. For she participated eagerly in all of the Shaker worship services wherever she went—and there were many others besides those on Sunday morning to which strangers were welcome. Her attitude toward the public gatherings was, understandably, a little less enthusiastic. "The world behaved well, and paid good attention to the speaking," she re-marked of one such service. "But whether one soul was aroused from their slumbers of death or not is more than I can tell."

However, when the Shakers were not inhibited by the presence of outsiders, their sense of release brought them much greater spiritual rewards. Although the New Lebanon ministry had recently discouraged the receiving of any spiteful messages from the spirits of departed members, sacred messages were still an important feature of their private worship services, and so was the receipt of spiritual presents like baskets of heavenly fruit. Throughout her diary, Sister Prudence kept reporting on the spiritual gifts so generously distributed at these Shaker gatherings no outsider could watch, as for instance:

> *July 13th* In the afternoon we . . . had a very good meeting. After some exercise the Angel Micalon delivered a short but solemn word exciting our minds to a spirit of true thankfulness for the gospel of Christ and Mother. At the close of the meeting we all received a beautiful dove of protection from the Holy Mount sent from Mother Ann. . . .

But the workaday world of spinning wool or milking cows was not neglected by Sister Prudence. She offers a wealth of specific details about the physical appearance and daily routine of each of the eight villages the traveling Shakers visited.

At Union Village near Cincinnati, she and Eliza visited the first family, inspecting their new house "and a very handsome house it is, built of brick and covered with slate." The second family had ninety-six members. The west family had a new mill house beside a dam with a "spinning machine for spinning wool which runs by the water; the number of spindles is 140, they spin 50 pounds of wool in a day & sometimes 70 pounds." Then:

> We went to see the cows. William McFarlon takes care of them. He has 60, all of the Durham breed. Their horns are very homely, but they are as fat as meadow moles. A number of them give each day a large pail of milk at a milking.

And:

> We went to see the elders' new carriage, that the brethren are making; called at the herb shop where Brother Abiathor was grinding. [The leaves are] run between two large cast iron cylinders turned by horse power, which bruised them pretty well. I suppose it is all sufficient, but it is not quite so fine as the brethren at the east grind it.

Then when the travelers arrived at the South Union Shaker community in Kentucky, covered nearly from head to toe with clinging insects that had to be removed with tweezers, they bathed, ate some watermelon, attended an excellent meeting, and the following morning:

> We have been taking a walk to see the shops and mound, or Cistern, that supplies three families with water which is brought half a mile underground from a never failing well. From this mound it is conveyed by aquaducts into the buildings.

After returning to Ohio, then proceeding northward to take a different route home to New Lebanon, Sister Prudence and her friends stopped outside of Cleveland. There they found the 160 local Shakers "not yet so well accommodated for buildings as they are in some places among believers . . . but it is, or will be a beautiful place after a little more improvement." Already the community had

> . . . a good mill but they had to dig thro' a solid rock a number of feet in order to get a good fall of water. We went downstairs into the wheel pit which was a real sight or curiosity to me; when ascending, I counted the steps, there were 62.

After a fearful crossing of Lake Erie, during which practically every passenger on their steamboat felt ill, Sister Prudence and her friends proceeded by train and stage to the western New York Shaker community of Groveland. There they broke their journey with a restful visit lasting only one night for "if we had staid any longer we could not have reached Watervliet until the Sabbath," and rather than risk missing a Sabbath meeting they chose to curtail their stay. Nevertheless, they managed to inspect the western village's new mill and meetinghouse, besides receiving "a new store of good gospel love and blessing to bring to our beloved friends at New Lebanon."

By canal boat and then by train, they went on to Albany, arriving on the second of October. From there a team of horses conveyed them to Watervliet, so close to their own village that they felt nearly home. "Yea, it was joy to my weary spirits to get once more among my dear gospel relations," Sister Prudence wrote, adding:

> Not that I have suffer'd any sense and spirit to blend with the world on my journey. Nay, that I have not done, neither have I felt the least inclination so to do; for they have nothing among the chiefest of them, that feeds or fills my soul in the least degree.

Secure in the strength of her own belief, and refreshed by several excellent meetings at Mother Ann's own former refuge, Sister Prudence and her party finally returned to New Lebanon "all alive and well" on the afternoon of October 6. There she wrote the final reverent passage of her diary, reflecting on the special privilege she had enjoyed of meeting so many believers in the West who were as much like Mother Ann's good children as her other Shaker brothers and sisters here at home. The final words of her 103-page manuscript are:

> *Even so let it be*
> *Thro time and eternity.*

❦ *Eleven* ❦

South Union

EVEN THE NAME was an affront to Dr. Rhea and his friends. South Union, the Shakers' southernmost community, was just about as far south as anybody could be in slave-owning Kentucky. In those parts, feeling ran strongly in favor of seceding from the Union if federal interference with the South's right to keep slaves could not be stopped.

But besides using such an unpopular word in their address, the Shakers actually had some black men, women, and children living on their property, and they treated them no differently from the way they treated any other of their believers. Dr. Boanarges Rhea, who owned a plantation a few miles away, kept telling all the gentlemen of his acquaintance that the whole lot of these religious riffraff ought to be chased north where they belonged.

Then, when the crisis between the North and South finally came to a head and the armies of both sides began fighting the Civil War, the Shakers seemed no better than traitors in the eyes of Dr. Rhea. With others of his neighbors, he wanted Kentucky to join the Confederate cause. However, there were also many people in Kentucky who wished to save the Union at all costs, and the state could not give its full loyalty to either camp. The opposing armies sought to settle the issue by force of arms. Unhappily for the peace-loving Shakers, their South Union settlement could hardly have been located more uncomfortably.

Running right through the center of their village was a state road connecting Bowling Green, fourteen miles to the northeast, with the town of Russellville, where Confederate supporters had set up a provisional government. Naturally this town was a prime target for the Union strategists. Another road bisecting Shaker land led directly to Fort Donelson on the Cumberland River and Fort Henry on the Tennessee. As if these militarily valuable routes were not sufficient reason for Shaker concern, skirting the southern edge of their property was the Memphis branch of the Louisville and Nashville Railroad, which prided itself on offering the fastest rail service in the South.

As a result, the Shakers not only had to contend with neighbors like Dr. Rhea who suspected them of treason, and with other neighbors who felt that they must secretly be supporting the rebels because they would not give up their traditional pacifist position to help the Northern cause. The serenity of their village was constantly broken when raiding parties and even whole battalions of troops galloped right through—or, even worse, stopped.

Within the first few months of the war, South Union's ordeal was already creating a new chapter in Shaker history. Realizing that the community's experience must be unique, Eldress Nancy Moore decided in August 1861 to keep a journal, and its first entry sets the tone for the whole document:

Aug 15 The Rebel Colonel Forest with a company of Cavalry eighty six in number, passed thro' our village from above; they had several small secesh flags flying at their horses ears; (we supposed to plainly show who and what they were.) They passed on very civilly and encamped at the head of our Mill pond.

We accommodated them with supper and breakfast, also furnished them with plenty of fruit, Apples, Peaches &c; without charge. . . . This Company purloined a few Cabbage heads, and a few melons from the west garden, otherwise they behaved as well as we could expect.

Despite this rather good behavior, it was immediately obvious to the Shaker brothers at South Union that exceptional precautions had better be taken. Soldiers notoriously took what they needed from the countryside where they were fighting, and although the Shakers had ample stocks of food and animals by virtue of their regular industry, they could not possibly supply whole armies without suffering shortages themselves. So the brothers began hiding their best horses and separating wagons into pieces, then putting the pieces in the most unlikely places.

Thus prepared, they felt moderately secure when they heard in October that two Confederate generals were sending agents into the neighborhood to round up all available horses and wagons. But the South Union community failed to reckon on the enmity of some of their neighbors. On October 29, Eldress Nancy reported that John McCutcheon, Jr., and his mother, "who are by no means friends to us," had led Confederate agents around the Shaker village pointing out where wagons and horses might be found. "Also, Doctor Rhea came up and done what he could to assist them in robbing us."

An elder from Mount Lebanon. Note the typical Shaker haircut LEES STUDIOS PHO-TOGRAPHERS THE SHAKER MUSEUM, OLD CHATHAM, NEW YORK

An eldress dressed in typical Shaker fashion THE NEW YORK PUBLIC LIBRARY PICTURE COLLECTION

From then on, military intrusions came thick and fast. The Shakers tried to adjust by allowing soldiers to camp on their property without any charge, even though their neat fields were trampled and their animal fodder was often stolen when they did so. If officers requested meals for their men, or blankets or coats, Shaker sisters politely offered to sell whatever they had available, and at first payment was usually made, although it might be in Confederate notes worth only seventy-five cents to the dollar. As the months passed, however, the sisters packed away all their nicest blankets and began to serve soldiers homemade sassafras tea and rye coffee as substitutes for the "good bought Tea and Coffee" they could no longer afford. Nevertheless, their sleep was often disturbed by "hideous yells" when troops stopped in quest of sustenance. So other measures had to be tried, as in January 1862 when the brethren tried to convince a troop of cavalry to move on to a tavern only about a mile distant for supper and lodging because an epidemic of measles was afflicting the Shaker village. But the soldiers showed no fear of catching the disease, and they threatened to break into the kitchen if food was not immediately provided for them. "When we found they would not be put off," Eldress Nancy wrote, "the Sisters got up and prepared supper for them as quick as possible."

The next morning the Shakers had better success. When "five armed Rebel marauders" demanded "cloth, Jeanes, Silk Kerchiefs or any other thing of the kind we might have for sale," the sisters were able to convince the soldiers that no such articles were on hand "to buy or to take by force of arms."

Still the Shakers were unable to avoid having their

ordinary routine completely disrupted. Faced by constant calls for quantities of food like six hundred pounds of bread, the sisters all but ceased their regular duties. The brothers, too, were mainly engaged in serving the military, most usually by chopping wood to fuel the soldiers' campfires. "As we look out of our windows," Eldress Nancy wrote one winter evening, "we see the Western portion of our little village, to all appearance a Barrack for soldiers. The fires blazing, the sparks flying in high winds, their shouting and wild cheering contrast strongly with the peaceful and quiet appearance which has always characterized this place."

Yet the calm manner of the Shakers obviously impressed the intruders. At least some of the men effusively thanked the sisters for taking such pains to feed them so well. One day, one of them gallantly told Sister Hannah, "Madam, I fear you will kill us with good victuals." She immediately replied, "Better that, than with a bullet." As Eldress Nancy approvingly commented, "This seemed to take him by the heart." But her sympathy did not extend to the villainous Dr. Rhea, who appeared later while the premises were still filled with soldiers:

He tauntingly said, Well, ladies, you have some new accessions to your family. I did not know till of late you were increasing so fast in numbers, and they all appear to be of the male order—I see no females among them. We let him pass on without any compliments.

Under the circumstances, Eldress Nancy could not resist taking pleasure when Dr. Rhea finally was treated to a taste of his own medicine. Because the Shakers clearly could not provide sufficient food from their own stock to feed so many men, Confederate agents combed the neighborhood seeking other supplies for the sisters to use in their cooking and baking. Dr. Rhea was ordered to provide butter and beef from his own stores, but he did not deliver it quickly enough to suit the officer in charge.

The result was that a dozen armed men appeared at the doctor's mansion, hitched up one of his wagons, and simply helped themselves to what they wanted from his kitchen storehouse. "It was rather a bitter pill for the old doctor to swallow," Eldress Nancy noted, "not withstanding he had so lately administered something of the kind to others." Then, when Dr. Rhea complained about the harsh way he was being treated, the Confederate agents "laughed and made sport of him."

But Dr. Rhea was to suffer more than this mild abuse, for in February 1862 federal troops entered Bowling Green. Throughout the rest of the war, Confederate raiders kept causing trouble, and control of strategic points shifted repeatedly, but the Union forces increasingly solidified their position. While the Shakers maintained their strictly neutral stand, they could not quite disguise their emotional leaning toward the Union side, mainly because of their distaste for slavery. And Dr. Rhea could not quite disguise his sympathy with the Confederacy.

Late in 1862, after some undisciplined Union troops burned practically all of the Shakers' wooden fences to keep their campfires going, and stole much of the community's remaining animal fodder in the bargain, Dr. Rhea came on another visit and "he professed to be very sorry to see our premises so abused." He did not appear to feel very sorry, though, and his sarcastic tone aroused the suspicions of two federal soldiers who rode up while he was talking. They demanded to know if the doctor was a Confederate sympathizer.

No, Dr. Rhea said, he was a friend to the Union, not an enemy.

That statement astounded the Shakers who heard it, but they tried to behave charitably and would not denounce the old man as a liar. Nevertheless, Eldress Nancy added, "Somehow the soldiers concluded it would be safe to take him into custody, and they required him to go with them to Russellville."

Apparently all that Dr. Rhea had to do there to secure his freedom was to swallow his previous feelings and swear an oath of allegiance to the federal government. Thenceforth, he troubled the Shakers no further. Yet the Shaker wish to live in peace with the whole human family was not to be granted for two more years. They tried to carry on with their normal occupations, as a Union captain noticed while his men were quartered there. He was particularly struck by the sight of Shaker brothers busily repairing a stone walk. "He said we ought to engrave in deep letters which never can be erased," Eldress Nancy wrote, "Laid in the Year of the Rebellion of 1863. While the people of the United States were at war fighting & killing each other the Shakers remained quietly at home improving their village."

But the South Union Shakers were far from untouched by all the carnage around them. When two unruly soldiers got into a brawl, the eldress herself used distinctly un-Shakerlike language to describe what happened:

This same Bostick who not long since threatened to let out Brother Urbans guts and to kill Lorenzo got into a scrape with a man by the name of Short and drawed a bowie knife on him. Another man by the name of White, Shorts brother in law, seeing this took out his pistol and fired at Bostick but missed his aim and hit Short in the head; he fell dead and never kicked.

Besides having their normally peaceful lives upset by such violence, the Shakers of South Union also suffered real hardship because of the war. From fire, theft, and the incidental damages inflicted by the thousands of men they fed, their village lost the prosperous look they had worked so hard to achieve. Toward the end of the war, they even ran short of food and firewood. Probably most serious in the long run, constant exposure to worldly ways spoiled the attraction of Shakerism for many of the younger believers. Elder John tried to warn them "in a very tender and affectionate manner" about the danger of indulging in "so much loud, boisterous, ungodly laughing and conversation." Nevertheless, the membership of the society steadily decreased.

Some of the young men who left the fold were trying to escape the possibility of having to put on a uniform and fight. During the earlier stages of the war, rumors that the Confederacy intended to draft even Shakers stirred several of the younger brothers to flee into Union territory. But then, in 1863, when South Union itself was fairly secure Union territory, the federal Congress in Washington passed a draft law that actually did seem to require registration for military service by all Shaker men in the appropriate age group. It was this emergency measure that brought the Civil War most directly to bear on the whole Shaker community, from Maine to Kentucky.

Until then the other Shaker villages had been able to carry on approximately as usual, although some of the more adventurous young brothers had been lured into leaving Shakerism to volunteer as soldiers. But these less than totally convinced believers would probably have run off anyway, sooner or later. In the case of more dedicated believers, the draft law posed a real test.

Ever since the American Revolution, the responsibility of Shaker men in time of war had been subject to two different interpretations. To the Shakers themselves, there was no question that their religious belief exempted them from any call to fight. Under no condition would they bear arms. But to various state authorities, the issue was not that simple.

Because Shakerism had been such a minor force during the early years of the country, none of the states had tried too hard to make Shakers serve in their militia. Where such efforts were made, the Shaker village involved was encouraged by the New Lebanon ministry to pay whatever was required to hire substitutes. However, with the passage of time it began to appear wrong for Shakerism to compromise its principles in this manner. New Lebanon ordered, instead, that no community should even pay money to aid any warlike purpose. Eventually, though, the legislatures of most of the states where Shaker villages were located passed laws recognizing the Shaker right to conscientious-objector status—and when any Shaker male faced military duty in any state that had not granted this special status, the common practice was for him to take refuge in some other Shaker village across a state line, where he would be safe from prosecution.

The federal action of 1863 posed a new and much more difficult problem. By this time, however, an extremely able man had succeeded to the top Shaker position as head of the New Lebanon ministry. He was Elder Frederick W. Evans, who had many unusual ideas about what the role of Shakerism ought to be. Instead of shunning worldly involvement in every possible way, he thought the Shakers should adapt themselves to new conditions whenever necessary. Under the stress of the Civil War draft threat, Elder Frederick gave a good example of his policy in action. He personally traveled to Washington to visit President Lincoln.

Elder Frederick brought a long and closely reasoned letter with him, setting forth the many grounds on which he thought the Shakers deserved complete exemption from the draft. Besides listing all the religious scruples that prohibited any faithful Shaker from lifting a gun, the elder added an ingenious new point for the President to consider.

After both the Revolution and the War of 1812, former soldiers had been granted various amounts of money from the national treasury as pensions or rewards. But there were a goodly number of veterans who became Shakers following their military service, and they had never collected a penny of the money due them. The amount the government still held in their names totaled $439,733, including interest, Elder Frederick calmly told Mr. Lincoln. Should the Shakers claim all this money, the elder said, it would cost the government rather more than it could gain from the military service of the hundred or so Shaker men currently eligible for active duty.

"Well, what am I to do?" President Lincoln asked Elder Frederick.

"It is not for me to advise the President of the United

States," the elder replied, according to his later recollection of the conversation. Then, as he remembered, Lincoln leaned back in his chair and smiled.

"You ought to be made to fight," Lincoln reportedly said. "We need regiments of just such men as you." Then he formally granted Elder Frederick's request.

Twelve

"Of course we like to keep up our numbers ..."

EVEN THE EARLY LIFE of Frederick Evans had been quite different from the usual Shaker's. Instead of spending his youth among God-fearing farmers in rural America, either in the children's quarters of some Shaker village or more likely exposed to bleak poverty as part of an unfortunate family, he had been born to well-off parents in England. And instead of moving to Shakerism after being disappointed in more conventional religious doctrines, he had been a convinced atheist during his early adulthood.

But the extraordinary career of this man, who became the most powerful influence on Shakerism throughout much of the second half of the nineteenth century, probably owed its basic direction to his unusual early experiences. Because his mother had died when he was only four years old, he had been taken in by an aunt and uncle who must have been remarkably set in their ways. Chadwick Hall, their country home, was operated with the help of eight or ten servants as the very model of a gentleman's farm. "Everything moved as if by machinery," Elder Frederick later recalled.

A small boy, no doubt extremely lonely after the loss of his mother and the unexplained disappearance of his father, must have seemed quite a nuisance to these prim relatives. As soon as they possibly could, in 1816 when he was just eight years old, they sent him away to boarding school. Their action was not as cruel as it might seem, for the English gentry often enrolled their sons in such schools at an early age, but Frederick Evans already had a strong nonconformist streak. He positively refused to study, and the headmaster called him the worst pupil in his whole experience. Within a few months, the boy was back at Chadwick Hall.

There Frederick spent most of the next four years with the servants, learning something about farming and nothing about books. When he was twelve, he was summoned unexpectedly into the parlor. There a man and a boy who seemed a few years his senior were seated. Fredrick could not remember ever having seen either of them before. His uncle brusquely spoke to him. "Frederick," he said, "will you go to America with these men who are your father and brother, or will you stay with us?"

From some of the hired hands in the barn, Frederick had heard a tune dating back to the time when British soldiers had gone off to fight the colonists rebelling on the other side of the Atlantic:

> *The sun will burn your nose off,*
> *And the frost will freeze your toes off;*
> *   But we must away,*
> *To fight our friends and our relations*
> *   In North America.*

That was all Frederick knew of the place he was being asked about, but he did not hesitate. "I will go to America with my father and brother," he told his uncle.

They sailed on a ship called the *Favorite*, and after a stormy voyage they stopped only briefly in New York before hiring a team to drive them and their baggage to the upstate town of Binghamton. Two other uncles had previously settled there, and Frederick soon met a flock of book-reading cousins who teased him for being so ignorant. "I made up my mind that I would learn to read, and *love* to read," he later wrote. During the next several years, he applied himself with such a will that he practically memorized the works of Plato and Shakespeare. "I also took up theology, and asked myself, why was I a Christian, and not a Mahometan or a follower of Confucius?—for I had read the Koran and the Bibles of all peoples that I could obtain."

The result was that he decided against all religion, but put his faith in radical politics. With his brother George, he founded a paper called *The Workingman's Advocate*, which attracted a small but loyal following by printing headlines like DOWN WITH MONOPOLIES. Frederick had to act on his principles, though, and not just write about them, so first he adopted a series of high-minded rules of personal conduct; then he began making plans for starting an ideal community based on "Socialistic-Communism." While seeking information about how he might best proceed, he visited New Lebanon in 1830.

He thought, before he went there, that the Shakers "were the most ignorant and fanatical people in existence." He had merely intended to observe the way they had organized their settlement. "But I was agreeably surprised," he wrote in his *Autobiography of a Shaker* nearly forty years later. He was so agreeably surprised and impressed by what he saw—and felt—that he stayed three months, then left only briefly to return to New York and astound his brother by announcing his conversion to Shakerism.

While George Evans went on to become one of the more widely known radical writers of the nineteenth century, Frederick rose to at least an equal eminence. His undeniable talents soon brought him to the top of the Shaker hierarchy, and by the Civil War his position as the "lead" in the New Lebanon ministry was formally accepted. By a happy accident of literary history, it is possible to tell in precise detail exactly how he went about exercising his influence because one of the outstanding journalists of the day did an expert job of interviewing him.

Charles Nordhoff, the Washington correspondent of the New York *Herald*, had decided early in the 1870's that the labor-union problems then just beginning to agitate the country were a dangerous symptom. He foresaw "a serious calamity" for the United States unless some new way was found to give its hired workmen a reasonable hope that by their own efforts they could achieve a measure of independence. During the nation's early years, any ambitious person had been able at least to dream of escaping a life of unending toil in the service of a selfish employer by going west. But the cheap and fertile western land that had served as a safety valve for poor city people was already running out, and Nordhoff wondered if a system of cooperative industry might possibly become the safety valve of the future.

So he determined to investigate the assorted varieties of voluntary communism that different groups had been trying. Besides doing a prodigious amount of reading about past experiments no longer available for firsthand study, he personally visited every existing commune whose location he could discover—a total of seventy-two, established by a dozen different societies, among them the Perfectionists of New York; the Harmonites of Pennsylvania; and the Separatists of Ohio. Since the Shakers were the oldest and in many other aspects the most successful of the American communes, he devoted fully one third of his 430-page book to them.

The book was called *The Communistic Societies of the United States*, and ever since its publication in 1875 it has been considered a classic example of good reporting. More timely a century after its first appearance than even its thoughtful author might have predicted, in its paperback reprinting it is required reading for many college courses in the 1970's. Despite its age and its solid content of fact, it gives almost as vivid a picture of the communes it describes as a contemporary television documentary. Here are Nordhoff's own words introducing the chapter about his stay at Mount Lebanon:

It was on a bleak and sleety December day that I made my first visit to a Shaker family. As I came by appointment, a brother, whom I later found to be the second elder of the family, received me at the door, opening it silently at the precise moment when I had reached the vestibule, and, silently bowing, took my bag from my hand and motioned me to follow him. We passed through a hall in which I saw numerous bonnets, cloaks, and shawls hung up on pegs, and passed an empty dining-hall, and out of a door into the back yard, crossing which we entered another house, and, opening a door, my guide welcomed me to the "visitors' room." "This," said he, "is where you will stay. A brother will come in presently to speak with you." And with a bow my guide noiselessly slipped out, softly closed the door behind him, and I was alone.

I found myself in a comfortable low-ceiled room, warmed by an air-tight stove, and furnished with a cot-bed, half a dozen chairs, a large wooden spittoon filled with saw-dust, a looking-glass and a table. The floor was covered with strips of rag carpet, very neat and of a pretty, quiet color, loosely laid down. Against the wall, near the stove, hung a dust-pan, shovel, dusting-brush, and a small broom. A door opened into an inner room, which contained another bed and conveniences for washing. Every thing was scrupulously neat and clean. On the table were laid a number of Shaker books and newspapers. In one corner of the room was a bell, used, as I afterwards discovered, to summon the visitor to his meals. As I looked out of a window, I perceived that the sash was fitted with screws, by means of which the windows could be so secured as not to rattle in stormy weather; while the lower sash of one window was raised three or four inches, and a strip of neatly fitting plank was inserted in the opening—this allowed ventilation between the upper and lower sashes, thus preventing a direct draught, while securing fresh air.

I was still admiring these ingenious little contrivances, when, with a preliminary knock, entered to me a tall, slender young man, who, hanging his broad-brimmed hat on a peg, announced himself to me as the brother who was to care for me during my stay. . . .

From then on, Nordhoff provided equally clear and detailed descriptions of every aspect of Shaker living, from the same open-minded standpoint. Noting that the hair of every brother "was cut in the Shaker fashion, straight across the forehead, and suffered to grow long behind," he avoided the common tendency to poke fun at this particular style just because it was unusual. But he never hesitated to voice his personal opinion about more significant matters. Admiring the "astonishingly bright and clean" floor of the meetinghouse, which looked brand new although it had been used nearly thirty years, he reported that besides sweeping and polishing the boards daily the Shakers also preserved them from scratches by wearing only especially soft leather shoes in this chamber. "They have invented many such tricks of housekeeping," he remarked, "and I could see that they acted just as a parcel of old bachelors and old maids would any where else, in these particulars—setting much store by personal comfort, neatness, and order; and no doubt thinking much of such minor morals."

First in a general review of Shaker practices both past and present, then in separate sections on each of the eighteen communities, Nordhoff offered a complete blueprint for anybody who might want to copy the Shaker model. "The Shaker family rises at half-past four in the summer, and five o'clock in the winter," he wrote, and he listed their mealtimes, outlined their work schedules, even dwelt on their laundry arrangements. A member of the Shaker settlement in Canterbury, New Hampshire, had invented a machine that could wash large quantities of clothing, he explained, and besides using such washing machines themselves, the Shakers sold them to hotels and various public institutions.

However, Nordhoff paid equal attention to the philosophy of Shakerism, which Elder Frederick willingly discussed with him. These conversations probably account for the book's continuing appeal to readers who have no intention of founding or joining a commune, partly because they give such a balanced statement of the advantages—as well as

147

the disadvantages—of the Shaker life style, and partly because they introduce such an interesting personality.

Elder Frederick was a tall man with brown eyes, a long nose, a kindly, serious face, and an attractive manner, Nordhoff noted, adding: "He is now sixty-six years of age, but looks not more than fifty." On this matter of the good health and unusually long life spans that had become remarkable among Shakers ever since their farms had begun yielding abundant harvests, the elder spoke with his typical directness. Regular habits and simple wholesome food practically guaranteed freedom from disease, he said. "I hold that no man who lives as we do has a right to be ill before he is sixty," he observed. "If he suffer from disease before that, he is in fault."

Concerning other significant features of Shakerism, Elder Frederick was equally positive:

> Every commune, to prosper, must be founded, so far as its industry goes, on agriculture. Only the simple labors and manners of a farming people can hold a community together. Wherever we have departed from this rule to go into manufacturing, we have blundered.

However, he was obliged to admit that the changing economy of the nation as a whole had inevitably changed Shakerism, too. Although the policy that each community should produce the greatest possible portions of its own needs still seemed wisest, in practice the growth of mass-production industries in the outer world had tempted the Shakers to buy items they had formerly made themselves:

> We used to have more looms than now, but cloth is sold so cheaply that we gradually began to buy. It is a mistake; we buy more cheaply than we can make, but our home-made cloth is better than we can buy; and we have

The Shaker Community at Watervliet, New York, with the North Family in front of their living quarters. Original photograph, published in the 1870's, is by Irving of Troy LEES STUDIOS PHOTOGRAPHERS THE SHAKER MUSEUM, OLD CHATHAM, NEW YORK

now to make three pairs of trousers, for instance, where before we made one. Thus our little looms would even now be more profitable—to say nothing of the independence we secure in working them.

Still, the temptation to buy worldly products was hard to resist, as was the temptation to keep acquiring more land even though there was not sufficient Shaker manpower to farm it and hired labor had to be found. But on one point of Shaker philosophy, Elder Frederick was inflexible. Nordhoff said that considering the "homeliness" of the typical Shaker building, "which mostly have the appearance of mere factories or human hives," he wondered whether the Shakers, if they were to build anew, would pay more attention to beauty of design.

"No," said Elder Frederick, "the beautiful, as you call it, is absurd and abnormal. It has no business with us. The divine man has no right to waste money upon what you would call beauty." In any future buildings, more attention might be paid to securing better light and heat because these might tend to improve health and comfort, but "What is the use of pictures?"

Most of the household ornaments prized by the outer world were merely dust catchers, Elder Frederick said. "You people in the world are not clean according to Shaker notions," he commented, nor did society at large satisfy another Shaker requirement—in that women were still treated as inferior to men. "Here we find the women just as able as men in all business affairs," he said, "and far more spiritual."

"Suppose a woman wanted, in your family, to be a blacksmith," Nordhoff suggested. "Would you consent?"

"No," Elder Frederick replied, "because this would

bring men and women into relations which we do not think wise." He was referring, he explained, to the Shaker requirement that the sexes be kept separate in every possible way to avoid not only any sinful private attachment but also to preserve harmony. "We have no scandal, no tea-parties, no gossip," he said.

With all their rules for acceptable behavior, and the constant watch every Shaker kept on the conduct of other brothers and sisters, it was not very difficult, Elder Frederick said, to make sure that the society did not accept any applicants whose motives were bad. "If one comes with low motives, he will not be comfortable with us," the elder added, "and will presently go away."

To provide new members, many of the Shaker families still were bringing up children put into their care, the elder said, even though experience had shown that hardly one in ten of those young charges eventually signed the Shaker covenant. The best recruits, he said, were men or women who came to Shakerism at the age of twenty-one or twenty-two, after already having had enough of the world to satisfy their curiosity.

"Of course we like to keep up our numbers," Elder Frederick said, "but of course we do not sacrifice our principles."

There, Nordhoff pointed out, was the very nub of the Shaker problem. For a steady decline was obviously reducing their membership, although most of the Shaker leaders were still hoping the trend would reverse. But from a high of about 6,500 in the 1840's, the number of believers in the East and in the West had shrunk to about 2,500 by the 1870's. At each of the communities Nordhoff visited, he did his best to gather population figures relating to the earlier peak period, as well as to the then-current situation, and it was upon his findings that most later references to the Shaker enrollment would be based. Yet clear as the signs of decline might seem to any outsider, among the Shakers themselves the evidence was usually just dismissed as a temporary setback.

From Elder Frederick on down, most of the elders rejected any suggestion that if the strict Shaker discipline were relaxed to allow members more personal freedom, the number of recruits might increase. One of the standard Shaker rule books—by now, there were several of these that were supposed to guide believers' behavior—showed the extent to which obedience was expected. "Not a single action of life," it said, lacked "a rule for its perfect and strict performance," and among the examples given were the rules for stepping first with the right foot in ascending a flight of stairs, folding the hands with the right-hand thumb above the left, and kneeling, then rising again with the right leg first.

Nevertheless, the spirit of individualism exemplified by Elder Frederick himself could not help having an effect on Shakerism. While he wrote books for worldly readers, and exchanged letters with famous contemporaries like Russia's Leo Tolstoy, and even took several trips to his native England, his followers, too, broke some old Shaker taboos.

When Nordhoff visited one of the Ohio Shaker villages, he found that for the past three years a weekly business meeting of the entire community had been held to give the younger members some opportunity for expressing opinions and influencing policy. As a result, more books and newspapers were being permitted as leisure reading. "We feel that we must do something to make home more pleasant for our young people," one of the local elders told the visiting journalist. Then Nordhoff described the business meeting he personally attended:

> [It] lasts an hour, and the "Elder Brother in the Ministry" presides. I saw some evidence that this meeting aroused thought. Any member may bring up a subject for discussion; and I heard some of the sisters say that one matter which had occupied their thoughts was the too great monotony of their own lives—they desired greater variety, and thought women might do some other things besides cooking. One thought it would be an improvement to abolish the caps, and let the hair have its natural growth and appearance—but I am afraid she might be called a radical.

Many other observers besides Nordhoff also noticed that Shakerism was growing more liberal, if not radical, under Elder Frederick's rule. For despite his own words insisting there could be no sacrifice of basic Shaker principles, there was indeed some basic change. Even on the central question of the Mount Lebanon ministry's power, the old rigidity no longer applied. When Elder Frederick decreed that vegetarianism was the most healthful diet, several colonies went right on eating meat—and some others compromised by setting separate tables for meat-eaters, or by merely banishing pork but not beef.

Another respect in which the traditional Shaker strictness was relaxed had to do with the observance of Christmas. Throughout the earlier periods, the only acceptable way of marking December 25 had been to spend the day in solemn prayer. However, by the middle of the 1870's, quite a different program was being introduced, and the journal of Elder Otis Sawyer at Sabbathday Lake in Maine tells how his community put the new policy into effect:

The suggestion to have a Christmas tree, prepared in fitting simplicity, as part of a Christmas Festival received the ready approbation of the Ministry and Elders. A Committee of arrangements was at once formed. . . . Each person in the family was required to present some one or more articles as they could spare or were able to prepare. The six sisters of the Committee worked very industriously. . . . The Elders only were allowed to see what was prepared for each individual's present, inspected and sanctioned them. Many persons in the family were interested in different ways to make contributions to aid in the festivities. The Pupils in the school wrote pieces and were learning to recite appropriate verses & songs. Many Mottoes from Christ's words were printed very beautifully. . . .

Then, following a Christmas morning worship service "of uncommon excellence," the arrangements committee labored the entire afternoon to complete their program, which began when the evening meal was finished:

Promptly at the specified time the doors were thrown open and the brethren and sisters entered to behold one of the most pleasant surprises that had ever met their expectant eyes. The Christmas tree was all ablaze with light from the thirty-six lighted candles systematically attached to the limbs while a great variety of articles, tastefully arranged, filled the tree to its utmost capacity to hold, while two good sized tables were loaded with presents of needful and useful articles more or less for every individual in the family. This innocent display with the sweet Christmas Carol chanted by six young sisters sent a thrill of delight mingled with love and joy through every heart.

The contrast between such simple pleasures and the less appealing greed of the outer world impressed many outside the Shaker discipline. One of these was William Dean

Howells, editor of *The Atlantic Monthly*, who wrote feelingly about "A Shaker Village" in the issue of June 1876:

> It was our fortune to spend six weeks of last summer in the neighborhood of a community of the people called Shakers—who are chiefly known to the world outside by their applesauce, by their garden seeds so punctual in coming up when planted, by their brooms so well made that they sweep clean long after the ordinary new broom of proverb has retired upon its reputation, by the quaintness of their dress, and by the fame of their religious dances. It is well to have one's name such a synonym for honesty that anything called by it may be bought and sold with perfect confidence, and it is surely no harm to be noted for dressing out of the present fashion, or for dancing before the Lord. But when our summer had come to an end, and we had learned to know the Shakers for so many other qualities, we grew almost to resent their superficial renown among men. We saw in them a sect simple, sincere, and fervently persuaded of the truth of their doctrine, striving for the realization of a heavenly ideal upon earth; and amidst the hard and often sordid commonplace of our ordinary country life, their practice of the austerities to which men and women have devoted themselves in storied times and picturesque lands clothed these Yankee Shakers in something of the pathetic interest which always clings to our thoughts of monks and nuns. . . .

Yet despite the sense of exceeding peace Howells felt whenever he remembered the long, straight Shaker street, with its severely simple buildings on either side and fragrant gardens stretching in every direction, he felt no longing to live there himself. An elder of the community had brought up this very subject.

"We want cultivated people—half the subscribers to

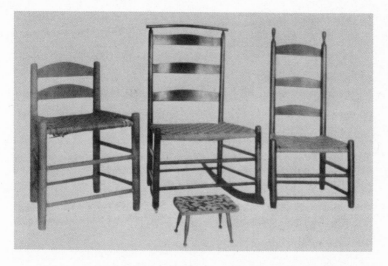

Several models of Shaker chairs THE NEW YORK PUBLIC LI-
BRARY PICTURE COLLECTION

The Atlantic Monthly—to come and fill up our vacant ranks," the elder had told the editor.

No, Howells replied, his readers were accustomed to a degree of worldly comfort that would not let them accept the required sacrifices easily. The Shakers might better search for converts, he advised, among the disappointed, the poor, and the friendless.

✤ Thirteen ✤

Caretakers of Children

ALTHOUGH EVERY SHAKER VILLAGE needed serious adult converts, fewer and fewer appeared as the years passed. Before Elder Frederick died in 1893, the community at Tyringham, Massachusetts, had to be sold, then North Union outside of Cleveland. In both cases, the few remaining members were moved to other settlements that were still managing to support themselves. Then Groveland in western New York had to close down in 1895.

Even though all of the villages were unmistakably declining now, those that continued to take children into their care hoped their communities might somehow survive. No matter if most of the children they had already raised had chosen to leave the fold, some Shakers could not believe this would continue to happen. The record kept by Sister Ada Cummings, who assumed charge of the girls' house at Sabbathday Lake early in the 1880's, proves her own faith.

"In commencing our duties as Caretakers of the Children," she wrote in her first entry, "we clean the *house* from garret to cellar, arranging things in *perfect* order, believing this to be necessary in order to become noble Members of the Church."

With Sister Prudie, who helped her, Sister Ada supervised the training of forty-seven girls during the two decades she held responsibility for the community's female youth. Most of the girls put in her charge were about ten or eleven years old when they were given over by some surviving relative. At least a few did not stay long, as the following entry indicates:

> *Sept. 12* A girl whose name is written in this book eloped with a hired man Wm Knight last night. They leave the state of Maine and go to New Hampshire where they are married. She was 15 years old last month.

Despite similar entries about runaways scattered through Sister Ada's notebook, she also recorded more encouraging facts, for instance:

> Clara is 16 years old today. She has been my girl 10 years and I am proud of her. May God keep her as safe in the future as she has been in the past.

And despite many notations about the sewing and laundry duties the girls were taught, the fast days they observed, and the quiet meditation they learned to practice, Sister Ada's record also included some evidence that innocent amusement was not altogether frowned upon. "I take the girls in the woods for a general romp after nuts," she wrote one October afternoon, "but do not find any." Then she added, "Elder Wm came out in the evening and brought a large basketful of nuts for them."

But Sister Ada's jottings only hint at what it must have been like to be brought up by the Shakers. Apparently this was a subject of some interest, however, because a number of more professional writers tried their hand at it. Among these was Kate Douglas Wiggin, whose *Rebecca of Sunnybrook Farm* became one of the best-loved children's books of the era. Hers was a sentimental Shaker tale entitled *Susanna and Sue.* A Maine resident during her childhood, Wiggin modeled her "Albion Village" on the Sabbathday Lake community. It was a highly romanticized depiction, however, with lovely apple blossoms seemingly always in bloom, a blue sapphire lake, and dazzling white buildings standing in the wide orderly spaces of their own farm and timber land. At first glance, this scene of perfect peace appeared deserted, but a closer look would show men out plowing in broad-brimmed hats, a boy with hair slightly long in back and cut in a straight line across his forehead carrying a milk can, and a quaintly clad girl beating a braided rug from a window.

To this serene hive of activity, a twenty-eight-year-old mother, Susanna Hathaway, has brought her young daughter, Sue. "I have left my husband for good and all," Susanna tells Eldress Abby, "and I only want to bring up Sue to a more tranquil life than I have ever had." What sort of unpleasant family problems these two are seeking to escape is not dwelt upon, but the young mother promises to work tirelessly if the Shakers will keep her and Sue.

"It is our duty," the eldress replies, "to receive all and try all." Then, in time, if Susanna should wish to be gathered into the faith, she would be expected to unburden her heart by confessing her past sins, and she would also be expected to signify her conquest of all ties of the flesh by giving Sue over to the sister in charge of the girls' order. Meanwhile, though, Susanna wil be able to keep the child with her. All that will be required of both mother and child now will be to show they are "pure and peaceful, gentle, easy to be entreated, and without hypocrisy. That's about all there is to the Shaker creed," Eldress Abby sums up, "and that's enough to keep us all busy."

But as near to paradise as Albion Village has struck both mother and daughter during their first hours there, they soon find unexpected difficulties. While Eldress Abby refrains from insisting that Sue's glorious golden curls must immediately be sheared off, at least they must be hidden under a plain Shaker cap. And the child's natural impulse to start a game with two Shaker children brings on an embarrassing scene.

When Sue's mother is escorted to the laundry house the next morning, the child notices a box that seems ideally suited for a playhouse. Within a few minutes, she lures other Shaker girls of her age into helping her transform it. Suddenly Eldress Abby is standing over them, saying firmly but not unkindly, "Morning's not the time for play. Run over to Sister Martha and help her shell the peas, then there'll be your seams to oversew."

Sue's mother is promptly told what has occurred. "Sue meant all right," Eldress Abby explains, "she was only playing the plays of the world, but you can well understand, Susanna, that we can't let our Shaker children play that way and get wrong ideas into their heads at the beginning."

"I see," Susanna says, and her desire to win Shaker peace is still so strong that she suggests later to her daughter that if any playing time is permitted, perhaps it would be better to play a Shaker kind of game, like "Mother Ann in Prison."

As the weeks pass, however, both mother and daughter

are increasingly distressed by the thought of having to separate. A letter from a relative finally gives Susanna some happy news. Her husband, it seems, has been so sobered by the departure of his wife and daughter that he has completely given up his old habits; he now goes to work regularly every day, and spends his evenings fixing their little house in the hope that his family may decide to return to him. Susanna finds herself wondering whether her true duty does not require keeping her marriage vows. As to the Shaker doctrine she has been trying so hard to accept, she finally reaches a wonderfully soothing conclusion.

Heaven is a big place and it all belongs to God, she decides. Thus no one group can set the rules for getting there. With no further qualms, she bids farewell to Albion Village, takes Sue by the hand, and together they joyously go back to the privacy of their own worldly home.

The fairy-tale qualities of Kate Douglas Wiggin's fiction would have disturbed any Shaker reader, though the novel's picture of Shakerism strikes the outsider as more than fair. The book's ending, which must seem happy to non-Shakers, would certainly have distressed convinced believers. From their viewpoint, a happier version of a similar story—and a much more accurate account of Shaker life as seen through a child's eyes—was contained in the actual diary of a thirteen-year-old Shaker boy.

Delmer Wilson, born in an isolated Maine village in July 1873, was brought to the Sabbathday Lake Shakers at the age of nine with his elder brother, Harry. Why their mother gave both her sons to the Shakers was not recorded. Perhaps like the fictional Susanna Hathaway, Dorcas Wil-

son had tried Shakerism herself; then, finding it unaccept-
able, she had left her boys to be cared for among people
who would feed and clothe them while she tried to discover
some way to earn their keep on her own. In any case, she
did not intend to abandon them permanently, as Delmer's
diary makes clear.

Understandably enough, he began his diary on a New
Year's Day, and although he wrote only a sentence or two
each evening, he told quite a lot in a few words, as a
sampling of his January entries indicates:

> *Saturday, January 1, 1887.*   It has been raining all day
> today and I had to stay to the barn. I am just five feet
> two inches & three quarters and I weigh 122½.

> *Sunday 2.*   We had a good meeting this after-noon and
> it has been very warm. I have got a calf that is just a
> week old tonight. It is Pansy's calf.

> *Friday 14.*   This forenoon Alvah and I lugged sixty
> quarts of water to the cows for it was so snowy that we
> did not let them out.

> *Friday, 28.*   School today. I write a composition en-
> titled, "Why not keep your mouth shut."

> *Saturday, 29.*   Today us boys was down to the barn and
> we put up a swing and had some fun.

The next day, Delmer finally mentioned his mother. His
brief remarks, together with some entries in the *Church
Record* kept about the whole community's activities, give at
least the basic outline of a touching story. Here is what he
wrote:

> *Sunday 30.*   Today I had a new cap, and I had a letter
> from my mother. This afternoon I see ten doves on the
> stable.

Monday 31. This morning a lot of the sisters was down to the barn to see the sheep and calves and they said that they were very fine ones. The sisters were down to the pond this afternoon and my mother came.

But Monday's *Church Record* makes the last three words less cryptic. "Harry Willson's mother is here," it reported, "and a man with her . . . [she] intends to take her boys home with her."

The next day, Delmer merely noted:

Tuesday, February 1. My mother went this afternoon and Harry went with her.

The *Church Record* again provides a little more information. "Dorcas Willson and man return home with her oldest son Harry Willson," it reported. Then, in just one more sentence, it offers two clues about why the woman whose last name the Shakers' record keeper repeatedly misspelled had achieved only partial success in her mission. "Dellie's mother would be pleased to take him too," the *Record* says, "but he is positive and says it is of no use to flatter him, he will not go from his best friends."

Throughout the rest of the winter, through sap-gathering time in the spring and then the planting of peas and potatoes, Dellie calmly recorded his daily activities with his friends. Not until a week before his fourteenth birthday did he mention his mother again:

Friday, July 1. Thof [a hired man] went mowing today. I raked it up. My mother was here today and Harry and the old man they came for any thing but good.

Once more, the *Church Record* provides a fuller explanation: "Dorcas Willson calls at the gate asking for her son

166

Dellie, but being refused she makes a big threat of what she will do. She sits in her carriage before the gate in the dreadful hot sun all the afternoon talking to Elder William and trying to get Dellie to leave home and go with her. But he does not think of such a thing. She does not leave until after supper."

After that failure, apparently Dorcas Wilson gave up. Her son's diary contains no further reference to her, but it does contain countless small bits of evidence that help to make Dellie's fondness for his Shaker friends understandable. Having lived among them from such an early age, he clearly cannot visualize any other style of life. Rather than feeling oppressed by the Shaker discipline, he appreciates the opportunity it provides for ensuring salvation. "We had a good meeting," he wrote repeatedly on Sunday evenings. "I spoke," he sometimes added, though with no hint about what he said.

Indeed the limited attention Dellie gave to religious matters in his diary shows how different Shakerism had become through the decades. In his experience, religion was mostly a matter for consideration at Sunday meetings. The fervor that had marked the earlier Shakers, to the extent that their whole lives were religiously oriented, had by now grown less enthusiastic. By no means had the remaining Shakers lost the faith that made them prefer their own separate existence above any worldly temptation, but they no longer actively sought spirit messages. At most Shaker villages, even the Sunday dancing had become sedate.

During this same period toward the end of the nineteenth century, other changes also occurred. One was in the schooling provided for children living in Shaker villages.

Originally, the Shaker philosophy had regarded too much learning as a dangerous thing, and education had been purposely neglected by the early leaders. Most of the training Shaker boys and girls had received was in skills like sewing or carpentry, rather than in traditional school subjects.

Around 1810, Mother Lucy Wright had decreed that some lessons in reading, writing, spelling, and arithmetic should be given to Shaker children. But the usual program had boys attending school just a few hours a week during three or four of the winter months; then, while they were busy with farm chores in the summer, similar lessons were given to the girls. In actual practice, the classes covered only the barest minimum of subject matter, and much more attention was paid to the teaching of obedience than to topics like geography.

Still, these Shaker schools, limited as they were, compared not too unfavorably with most rural education of the time. In fact, some townships thought the Shakers were doing such a good job of teaching the three R's that arrangements were often made for sending other youngsters who lived with their own families to attend Shaker classes. Why local authorities tended to admire Shaker teaching methods can be gathered from a report made by a town selectman after he visited the classroom at Sabbathday Lake in 1883. His report starts:

> This is a model school—whispering is seldom seen and in all movements the same good discipline prevails. While all the classes show a fair knowledge of their studies, special attention is given to the rules of reading, writing, spelling. . . .

But the Sabbathday Shakers were moving with the times, as was indicated by another part of the report: ". . . and in map drawing this school will take first place." For by the 1880's, the strictly moral Shaker reading manuals, containing page after page of rules about proper behavior, were being replaced by ordinary textbooks. Such subjects as "Elements of Botany" were being introduced. Lessons in freehand sketching and singing in harmony were being added to the curriculum.

There were even concerts at regular intervals, when the students sang musical pieces that would have been condemned a few decades earlier for their worldly tone. Other forms of recreation that now seemed quite harmless were also encouraged. The girls were helped to plan and grow flower gardens, the boys played ball or marbles. Shaker teachers gradually began to spend small sums from their educational funds for such formerly forbidden treats as peppermint candy sticks.

All this bending of old rules was quite ironic. Comparatively recently, the Sabbathday leadership had been vigorously struggling to gain the allegiance of children like Delmer Wilson. Some decades earlier, any Shaker youth who thought of leaving a Shaker community had been made to suffer a terrible ordeal. Encouraged by the elders, other members would surround the potential dropout, shouting, "Woe! Woe! Woe!" and stamping their feet to chase away evil spirits threatening the would-be backslider with eternal damnation. This ceremony was known as "the warring gift," and it must have frightened many who were forced to endure it. But although fear still kept some Shakers from going out into the world, the policy of trying to compel youthful conversions was gradually stopped. Then, at several villages, the former children's quarters became quite conventional boarding schools.

In rural areas, where the general level of education was not high, the change was actually fostered by non-Shakers. Parents, or guardians who had charge of orphans, somehow got the impression that they could secure a sound religious training for their youngsters by sending them to a Shaker school. They had no very clear idea about what Shakerism entailed, but the point was unimportant because they had no intention of giving the children up permanently. What they did know about the Shaker habits of neatness and industry made them want these traits taught to their children, and they were willing to pay a fair sum for such lessons. Since many of the traditional Shaker industries were failing, the Shaker leadership could hardly help welcoming this new opportunity.

Eldress Anna White, who now directed the largest remaining Shaker family at Mount Lebanon, was particularly energetic as a schoolmistress. She even had a prospectus printed for parents of the girls who might attend her classes. In this little folder she showed how far Shakerism had departed from the strict outlook of its earlier days. On the back page, describing the terms upon which students would be accepted, it set the annual fee for attendance from October through June (with a two-week recess at Christmas) at $200, and the only other important stipulation was: "Children will be required to attend our religious meetings. Those mentally or morally deficient will not be received."

However, most of the folder might have been describing

a school kept by Quakers or any other moderately unworldly religious denomination:

AIM

To make a "Perfect woman nobly planned.
To bless, to comfort and command."
PRACTICAL CHRISTIANITY WILL BE TAUGHT BOTH BY
PRECEPT AND EXAMPLE.

CURRICULUM

English and Industrial Branches.
Nature Study.
English Literature.
Elementary Music.
Bible Study.
Pupils fitted for College if desired.

INDUSTRIAL DEPARTMENT

Here are taught hand and machine sewing, plain knitting and crocheting. With help of instructors each girl will learn to keep her wardrobe in repair. All will assist in the baking and cooking department and in duties about the house, strength and adaptability being considered. The gathering and preparing of fruits and the cultivation of flowers form an important feature.

ADVANTAGES

LOCATION among the beautiful Berkshire Hills.
HYGIENIC CONDITIONS perfect; healthful recreations encouraged.
CAREFUL ATTENTION given to moral as well as mental and physical development.
VARIED AND NUTRITIOUS DIET A SPECIALTY.—The school being on a large farm, fruits, vegetables, dairy products, with whole wheat bread and all the important cereal foods form the diet.
A HOME LIFE, sweet, pure, and natural, where prevails the spirit of the Golden Rule.

171

DRESS

No uniform dress required. Simplicity in make, modesty in appearance and durability in material the chief requisites. All articles to be laundried should be particularly plain and simple. No jewelry or feathers allowed.

❧ *Fourteen* ❧

To the Last Man

ELDRESS ANNA had certainly not wavered in her own Shaker faith. With Eldress Leila Taylor, another of the leaders of the Mount Lebanon community, she wrote a book in 1905 addressed to the world at large. *Shakerism, Its Meaning and Message* appeared at a time when the Shaker ranks had been reduced to about a thousand members, and in effect, it was a sort of last appeal, like the song of a dying swan. Yet these devout believers calmly told their readers:

> Shakerism presents a system of faith and a mode of life, which, during the past century, has solved social and religious problems and successfully established practical brotherhoods of industry, besides freeing woman from inequality and injustice. To this there must be added that it has banished from its precincts monopoly, immorality, intemperance, and crime, by creating a life of purity, social freedom and altruistic industry. A system that has rendered such a service to mankind merits attention from all thoughtful people, whatever may be their position in life.

In short, the world would do well to study the Shaker experience—and learn from it.

To some extent, though, the two eldresses unwittingly misled the general public. Their own milder and more tolerant version of Shakerism made them gloss over the frenzy that had moved the early Shakers. Instead, perhaps because of their own increasing exposure to worldly phenomena like romantic fiction and, more importantly, the women's rights movement, they wrote about Ann Lee in words that strangely mingled the style of Kate Douglas Wiggin with the sentiments of Susan B. Anthony. "Useless your prayers, O little Ann!" the Shaker eldresses solemnly exclaimed. "Woman, in your day, had but one life before her, and at an early age Ann was married to Abraham Stanley, a blacksmith like her father. . . ."

Then, after telling their romanticized history, these two gentle and well-meaning women ended with a cry in favor of preserving the "good old careful ways."

The opening decades of the twentieth century could hardly have been a less receptive era for their appeal. To Americans at this time progress was the byword. City buildings were stretching skyward; populations of small towns were growing with unprecedented speed. Vast steel mills, oil refineries, and other factories increasingly changed the landscape. How could the quaint handcraft society of the Shakers have any meaning or message for a modern industrial giant like the United States?

Even the remote rural backwaters where most of the Shaker settlements were located had already felt the pressures of the new civilization. Since the Civil War, the nation's whole economy had altered so radically that the poorest farm wives scarcely thought of making their own soap any more when they could buy what they needed so cheaply. The neat fences the Shakers built around their property could not keep them from being affected by the same sort of influences. Although Elder Frederick had understood that buying cloth, instead of weaving it, had hurt the Shakers in the long run, he still had not been able to go back to the old system.

Whether or not the Shakers liked to admit it, the main reason their policy of producing most of their own needs had worked as well as it did during the early 1800's was that much of rural America was living in approximately the same manner. If a Shaker family could earn several hundred dollars by selling seeds, that was all it required to purchase those few items it wanted from the outer world. But when the family found that its own labor was, in effect, being wasted because there were increasing numbers of items it could buy more cheaply than it could produce, it could no longer continue what amounted to a barter arrangement with its neighbors. Like everybody else, the Shakers had to make more money so they could pay for all the new items on their shopping lists, and toward this end they had to concentrate their labor on those activities that seemed most likely to yield the greatest profit.

As a result, the Shakers had to give more attention to business matters. In some of their economic decisions, Shaker family trustees were extremely sensible. Since certain families had already built special shops or developed special skills, they embarked on their own brand of mass production. At Mount Lebanon, a chair factory produced chairs by the thousands to fill all Shaker needs as well as provide seating for worldly households. Canterbury in New Hampshire made and sold clothes-washing machines to such varied customers as Willard's Hotel in Washington, D.C., the Nova Scotia Hospital for the Insane, and the Pullman Palace Car Company. The superintendent of the Erie Division of the Pullman Company sent the Shakers a testimonial letter reporting that its machine had been in constant use for four years, "washing an average of 25,000 pieces per month, all that time without any repairs worthy of mentioning; which I consider a remarkable record, our work being all large pieces, sheets, pillowslips and towels."

Despite the fine Shaker reputation, though, and the careful management of some of its business operations, toward the end of the 1800's it became apparent that some Shaker brothers had very poor judgment when it came to land investments. There was a series of unsuccessful land-buying ventures, highlighted by an absolute fiasco in Florida.

In 1894, a small group of Shakers from chilly Watervliet in upstate New York journeyed south with the aim of establishing a new community in the "salubrious" climate of southern Florida. Brother Benjamin Gates was the leader of the group, and he had obviously heard not only about the healthful warmth of the climate but also about the rising market in Florida real estate. He thought the Shakers might make a fortune by picking out some inexpensive property that would eventually be worth millions—and that while they were waiting, they could enjoy the sunshine and earn their keep farming. But while Brother Benjamin looked around for a likely tract, Brother Andrew Barnett sent an unhappy letter back to New York. "When I see the greed of money step in and engross our whole attention," he wrote, "I begin to think we have forgotten the primary object of our exit into Florida."

Elder Frederick W. Evans. Original photograph taken by
Irving of Troy LEES STUDIOS PHOTOGRAPHERS   THE SHAKER
MUSEUM, OLD CHATHAM, NEW YORK

Nevertheless, Brother Benjamin finally selected seven thousand acres, for which he agreed to pay a land-development company the large sum of $94,500. When it soon became clear that most of the tract was either lake or swamp, with the rest covered by dense vegetation, the sum began to seem even larger. But the band of a dozen Shaker immigrants diligently started to work, clearing and building. By 1901 they had fenced about a thousand acres and had nine hundred cattle in the enclosed section, and they also had set out hundreds of orange, peach, apricot, and persimmon trees.

Brother Benjamin thought, though, that pineapple might be a better money crop, so he sent to Cuba for several thousand plants. Within five years the small community was selling three or four hundred pineapples a week. "The Shakers have an established reputation for furnishing only the best of everything," a local editor wrote, "and their pineapples are fully up to this standard."

For about five years, the Florida Shakers kept sending encouraging reports back to Watervliet. Bananas had been added to their plantation, they told their friends, and they had even discovered an unexpected source of income in their swamp, having recently sold a ten-foot alligator hide for $18.75.

Then a severe frost killed many of their trees during the winter of 1909. Hail damaged much of what had been spared. Facing the loss of most of their investment, the Shakers inquired further and found that most knowledgeable people thought fruit farming could be only a marginal operation in the area they had chosen because of the frequent vagaries of the weather. Brother Benjamin suggested they concentrate thereafter on selling lumber.

However, his companions had become increasingly discouraged, and one by one they departed northward. By 1911, only four Shakers remained in Florida, and they had the misfortune to become involved in a sensational newspaper story. A woman who had worked for them before having to enter a tuberculosis sanitorium had returned in the last stages of the disease, and she died among the Shakers under circumstances that led the local sheriff to charge them with "mercy killing." The case was finally dismissed, but the last of the Shakers left Florida soon afterward. With no more taste for discussing their mistakes than anybody else, the Watervliet community never mentioned how much hard-earned capital this ill-fated venture had cost them, but the figure must have been substantial.

Although the Florida fiasco was probably the most expensive of the Shaker losses, it was by no means the only case where they suffered by investing in land. Being farmers at heart, they could not help feeling that the best and safest place to put their money was in ever-larger tracts of property. If they had been able to let all this land sit idly while its value inevitably increased, the Shaker story might have taken quite a different turn. The skyrocketing prices of the past several decades might have made the most unworldly society of millionaires in American history.

But prosperous as they seemed during their heyday, the Shakers were never rich enough to put aside large sums for long-term investments. They had to earn a regular income to pay their bills. Their expanding acreage, instead of helping toward this end, actually hurt them financially. It placed practically every Shaker family in a vicious circle where hired hands were needed to work the extra land and the money that had to be spent on wages reduced the possibilities of making a profit. For like most other farmers, even the frugal Shakers could make a reasonable living out of agriculture only if they did not count their own dawn-to-dark labor as a dollars-and-cents cost on their yearly balance sheets. The more cash they spent for hiring helpers, the less chance they had to end the year with any surplus.

If the Shaker land had been rich prairie stretching, flat and fertile, as far as the eye could see, the problem could have been solved. New reaping machines, mechanical prodigies that did the work of dozens of men, were revolutionizing agriculture out in the Great Plains states. But the Shaker property, picturesque as its rolling hills and rocky outcrops might be, did not lend itself to the new farming techniques.

If a constant stream of strong young converts had kept replenishing the Shaker ranks, there still might have been some hope of staving off financial crisis. Instead, the average age of the remaining Shaker brothers was the only figure that showed an increase, and as the most elderly among them succumbed to illness and death, the disproportionate number of women that had marked the Shaker membership since the Civil War became ever more apparent.

Despite the efforts of nineteenth-century feminists like Elizabeth Cady Stanton and Susan B. Anthony, women obliged to earn their own living still faced great discrimination during the opening decades of the twentieth century. Their job opportunities were limited, and the rate of pay they could expect was generally half or less of what the going wages were for male workers. So the security Shakerism seemed to promise kept attracting some females.

Apart from the economic forces that were slowly disintegrating every Shaker community, some widely held ideas were probably a more important factor. Even at the height of its influence, Shakerism had had to contend with the typical American attitude of brash self-confidence. Back in the 1840's, an English visitor of the socialist persuasion, asking some city workmen why they were not joining the Shakers, had been told:

> We Americans love liberty too well to join such Societies as these. What are they but pure despotisms, where all are subject to the will of one man, a few leaders, or even a woman? Are these not places opposed to science and all improvements? We Americans are a go-ahead people, not to be confined anywhere or stopped by anything.

Such sentiments were even more widespread in the 1920's. Although the frontier days were over, the ordinary citizen still cherished dreams of somehow striking it rich. "Two chickens in every pot," Herbert Hoover promised when running for President in 1928, "and a car in every garage." That any free American should voluntarily give up every prospect for personal advancement could only seem ridiculous in this kind of political climate. And the utter nonsense of such a notion was multiplied to complete absurdity by the now obvious fact that such a sacrifice would be made in order to join a dying religion.

For there could no longer be the slightest doubt that Shakerism was dying. In 1908, the village at Shirley, Massachusetts, had closed. By 1910, the last of the four Ohio communities had been abandoned, along with Pleasant Hill in Kentucky. The few dozen surviving Shakers from all of these settlements moved to the last remaining outpost in the West, at South Union, Kentucky.

But South Union survived only until 1922, and by then the villages at Enfield, Connecticut, and Harvard, Massachusetts, were also gone. In 1923, Enfield, New Hampshire, was added to the sad list. Out of eighteen once-thriving communities, only six were still operating.

Nobody could imagine they were thriving, though. With their manpower reduced almost to the vanishing point, the main burden of supporting these half a dozen vestiges of the past had shifted to the aging women who made up most of their remaining population. The men's workshops were being locked up, one after another. The gift shops upon which the surviving villages were depending more and more for their support were gradually taking on the look of a church bazaar, featuring such items as homemade aprons and baby sweaters.

Even without the Great Depression of 1929, the last handful of Shaker villages would have been hard pressed to keep going on the proceeds of their little shops. Over the years, each village had sold parcels of land to pay for necessary improvements like a new roof for an old meetinghouse, or a new barn to replace one gutted by fire. But they still owned substantial amounts of property, which they hesitated to sell because it comprised their only real wealth, but which they were obliged to maintain under increasingly difficult circumstances.

Once their own brothers could have easily repaired broken shingles, but now villages had to pay hired workmen to do such essential chores. In the past, they had proudly refused to apply for exemption from taxes on the grounds of their religious commitment, but they had usually met their self-imposed debt to the larger community without actually paying any money. Shaker brothers had repaired local roads, or Shaker sisters had taught local youngsters, in a barter arrangement that admirably suited all parties concerned. However, now the Shakers could no longer pay their taxes this way, and the appeals for relief they were obliged to make met varying responses.

In 1932 the settlement at Alfred, Maine, had to close. Then in 1939 the sacred ground at Watervliet, New York, where Mother Ann herself had lived, was sold. A park, an airport, and a shopping center were carved out of the property, but at least the shells of a few of the old buildings were preserved by a state home for the aged. In 1947, Mount Lebanon, the home of the supreme Shaker ministry ever since Father Joseph Meacham's day, was also sold, in this case to the operators of a school and a summer camp.

That left only Hancock, Massachusetts, a few miles from Mount Lebanon, and the two more distant colonies at Canterbury in New Hampshire and Sabbathday Lake in Maine. Hancock, where the ministry moved, lasted until 1960, when the hard decision to sell this valuable site in the Berkshire Mountain resort area was finally announced.

Then only Canterbury and Sabbathday Lake remained. These two communities had been faring rather differently. At Canterbury about a dozen elderly women were still living in picturesque surroundings where three hundred Shakers had once operated a sawmill and raised sheep, besides producing the famous Shaker washing machines. But because of its location, about twelve miles from the New Hampshire capital of Concord and in the heart of the White Mountains, the Canterbury Shaker Village had long been a favorite visiting spot for summer vacationers. Possibly it was this worldly contact over so many years that had tended to relax some Shaker standards more than had been the case at other villages. For despite Canterbury's continuing strictness in religious matters, the community had gradually taken on some of the aspects of a Victorian summer resort. Croquet was played on the lawns, and flowery rugs and wallpaper contrasted with the severe simplicity of other Shaker living quarters. From gift-shop sales to summer visitors, the surviving women seemingly supported themselves quite comfortably.

Sabbathday Lake was much more austerely and traditionally Shaker. Thanks to the fruit-growing talents of its last surviving brother, it still had a thriving apple orchard. It had only recently sold its own herd of registered Guernseys, when the community realized it was spending more on grain to feed its cows than it made by selling milk. Nevertheless, until 1961 Sabbathday almost gave the impression that time had stopped there.

Then, in 1961, the last Shaker man died. Although he was eighty-eight and had been growing a little feeble during recent years, he had not stopped working until his final illness. That he served his faith with such remarkable diligence should hardly be surprising, for the brother who outlasted every other had already been a strong believer during his boyhood. His name was Delmer Wilson.

His death in one sense marked the end of the long Shaker saga, for now the nation's oldest and most extensive test of voluntary communism had definitely failed. Yet in another, and probably an even more important way, Shakerism was still very much alive. Even while the last remaining villages had been struggling to keep going, a new chapter in the Shaker story had already begun.

✦ *Fifteen* ✦

Revival

A SCHOOLTEACHER and his wife stopped to buy a loaf of homemade bread. A stockbroker found some old farming tools in the barn of the country estate he had just bought. From these small beginnings, a great revival of interest in Shakerism had been gradually developing over the past several decades.

The teacher was Edward Deming Andrews, a shy man of scholarly leanings who taught American history at the Scarborough School, a private academy near the Hudson River about thirty miles north of New York City. He and his wife, Faith, enjoyed spending their summers in the mountains of western Massachusetts. There, in 1923, the first omen that pointed toward a different Shaker future might have been observed.

Andrews was twenty-nine when he happened to stop at Hancock to try a loaf of Shaker bread. "A new world opened on that memorable day," he wrote thirty years later, in the introduction to his definitive history of Shakerism, *The People Called Shakers*. For bread had led to chairs, and furniture to other artifacts, until the whole Shaker experi-

ence came under the careful study of this dedicated re-
searcher.

More than merely an able scholar, Andrews was an en-
thusiast, and so was his wife. With the zeal of explorers
who had discovered a priceless treasure, they began by
working together on *Shaker Furniture*. Published in 1937,
this book soon created ripples of excitement among collectors
of antiques. A quarter of a century later, it was still being
given almost complete credit for turning a previously over-
looked category of woodcraft into valuable collectors' items.

The credit should probably be shared with a stockbroker named John S. Williams. During the years immediately following the Wall Street crash of 1929, this
young investment adviser found cause for selling his collection of Audubon bird prints and also his Georgia plantation. Then, around 1935, he bought another rural retreat
on a few thousand acres of New York farmland in the
Berkshire foothills, and being a born collector, he started
another collection—of old farm implements like those he
had first come upon in his own barn.

Since his property was only about a dozen miles from
Mount Lebanon, one of his earliest tool hunts took him to
the large Shaker barns there. At the time, John Williams
was thirty-five and Eldress Emma Neale was eighty, but
they quickly became friends. They had an obvious common
interest, for he wanted to buy such Shaker relics as a
blacksmith forge that had not been used for several decades,
and she was willing to part with unused equipment in
exchange for funds that might support her community
another few years. Beyond the pure business matter of
buying and selling, though, they had a more important
bond. John Williams could not help confiding his feeling

that a collection like his might have real historical value someday. And Eldress Emma could not help confiding her hope that authentic Shaker possessions would not be lost or scattered aimlessly when the last community closed its doors, as might well happen within the foreseeable future. "You know, Mr. Williams," the eldress predicted to her new friend one afternoon, "*you* are really going to start a Shaker Museum."

Eldress Emma was quite right. In 1940, she was the guest of honor at the private opening of the first exhibit—a complete Shaker blacksmith shop restored on the Williams grounds in Old Chatham, twelve miles from its original site near New Lebanon. The fever for collecting other Shaker-made items had completely infected John Williams. He traveled to all the remaining settlements, making friends with gentle old ladies and offering them cash for discarded school desks or cobblers' benches. He became a familiar figure at country auctions where genuine Shaker chairs or trestle tables might come up for sale.

But World War II interfered with his plans for expanding his museum. Finally, in 1950, when his collection had grown to include thousands of items, a way of carrying out Eldress Emma's prediction was evolved. A non-profit foundation was set up under the laws of New York State, and most of the Williams collection, plus six acres of land, was deeded to it. Then the nation's first Shaker Museum officially opened.

Eldress Emma did not live to see the museum completed, but she would certainly have marveled at what had been accomplished. In a peaceful rural setting with the trim order of a typical Shaker community, a cluster of barn-red and white frame buildings contain such a range of tools, furnishings, and other ingenious products that even a Shaker eldress of the twentieth century might be amazed. For during the gradual decline of all of the villages, their workshops had inevitably lost their neat look. Dust, that enemy of every Shaker, had settled over broom-tying machines and herb presses. Unused water mills had gathered cobwebs. But now each wheel and pulley has been polished, even the normal grit of a metal forge has been cleaned away, and the resulting immaculate display probably helped substantially to create the new impression of Shakerism that spread among the general public in the decades following the Second World War.

For the Shaker Museum at Old Chatham soon inspired other similar efforts. Two, widely separated geographically, were housed in actual Shaker buildings, and both owed their existence to the same new surge of admiration for Shakerism.

The wife of the editor of the *Berkshire Eagle*, a newspaper published in Pittsfield and widely read throughout western Massachusetts, Mrs. Lawrence K. Miller could remember when the Hancock Shakers had been ridiculed by some of their neighbors. When the last of the Shakers at Hancock decided in 1960 that their property must be sold, Mrs. Miller immediately went to work. She called dozens of influential citizens and told them she needed their help to save a valuable historical site. She soon had formed a committee of thirty-three pledged to contribute toward buying the Shaker village.

But the Shaker price was a quarter of a million dollars, which Mrs. Miller had to admit was reasonable for a choice parcel on the main highway between Pittsfield and Albany, New York. She knew that prospective motelkeepers might

189

willingly invest such a sum without even haggling, but her committee would never be able to meet a price of this magnitude. Nevertheless, she went to see the Shakers, and after she told them what she had in mind, they unhesitatingly cut their price—in half. This would be the Shaker contribution to a project they could heartily approve of, they explained, because it would provide such a fitting memorial to Shakerism.

She soon raised part of the required sum, borrowed the rest, and then as president of the non-profit corporation operating Hancock Shaker Village, she had the satisfaction, by the early 1970's, of seeing more than forty thousand visitors strolling through restored Shaker buildings and gardens every summer.

By then, even larger numbers of tourists were stopping at Pleasant Hill in Kentucky, where the warmer climate permitted year-round operation. Shakertown there had been deserted for nearly half a century when Earl Wallace, a retired oil-company executive, had the idea of restoring it and opening it as a museum. With the help of James L. Cogar, a former curator at the colonial restoration in Williamsburg, Virginia, he raised sufficient money to get started. Next they applied for a loan of $2 million from the Economic Development Administration in Washington, on the grounds that Shakertown as an educational and tourist attraction would give the depressed economy of the whole area about twenty-five miles southwest of Lexington a much-needed boost.

As soon as the loan was approved, local craftsmen went to work reproducing Shaker furniture while other workers repaired buildings and installed modern plumbing and electricity. For an additional feature of this Kentucky restoration was overnight accommodations where visitors could have modern comforts in an authentic Shaker atmosphere. In 1970, more than 65,000 guests took advantage of this novel opportunity.

Several other original Shaker colonies were also restored or remodeled to a lesser extent, and opened smaller museums. Only those Shaker buildings irretrievably lost by fire—or put to specialized use by previous purchasers, including schools, religious orders, and institutions such as homes for the aged—escaped being wholly or partly converted into exhibition galleries. During the same period, a number of general historical museums either started or enlarged collections of Shaker relics. However, like Old Chatham, they all tended to mislead many visitors.

For the new picture of Shakerism they provided was, unavoidably, a little unreal. Even those exhibits on actual Shaker premises where a few Shakers were still living could give only a part of the truth about Shakerism, and it was the most appealing part. Charles Dickens had heard a grim tone in the very ticking of a Shaker clock, and many other outsiders who saw the Shakers at the height of their experiment called them "crazy people." But during the long years of the religion's decline, most of the Shaker peculiarities had been discarded. Their utter silence at work, their frenzy at worship had been replaced as far as the outer world could tell with a remarkably calm yet cheerful demeanor. "Gentle" was the word most commonly used to describe the Shakers of the twentieth century.

These more recent recruits willingly admitted that they had changed some of the old Shaker ways. Why should that be surprising? They asked the question with a slight defensive tone. For if the whole world had changed so much, wasn't it only logical that Shakerism should adapt to new conditions? It was really provoking, Sister Mildred Barker would tell a visitor at Sabbathday Lake, it was provoking that an otherwise sound historian like Edward Deming Andrews could imply there had been no real Shakers after 1870.

Still, the plain fact was that practically every Shaker building, furnishing, and tool put on display during recent years had been produced by the old Shakers. "To Shakers today," Sister Mildred herself had said, "the pride taken in the accomplishments of their forerunners is tinged with some little regret—a regret not untouched by humor—that so many claim to understand or even to have developed expert knowledge in the field of Shaker arts and handcrafts, who have never developed any understanding of the spirit which produced them."

Sister Mildred spoke these words in accepting an award, "On behalf of all Shakers, living and dead," in 1965 from the Catholic Art Association of Albany, New York. She gently chided outsiders who looked at a Shaker chair and saw the material object as an end in itself. "They fail to see it as the product of a particular way of looking at the world," she explained.

So even the inanimate evidence of an unadorned Shaker cabinet would mislead most visitors to Shaker museums. For changing standards of style had exalted severely simple furnishings during recent decades, in preference to the ornate fussiness of what was fashionable when anonymous Shaker carpenters were making their furniture. It was simply not true that some superior aesthetic judgment had motivated the Shakers. On the contrary, the spirit that had moved them had demanded nothing less than strict obedience to the dictates of their Shaker elders.

By a firm rule established at Mount Lebanon, no Shaker craftsman could ignore specific restrictions. No carving, no ornamental molding, was allowed to express any personal feeling. All bedframes were to be painted green. Not even initials could indicate the identity of the individual who worked on any particular item. Instead of being a visible expression of a man's or sometimes a woman's own way of looking at the world, every Shaker artifact was a symbol of the almost complete sacrifice of individual creativity.

Then how could the painstaking craftsmanship of virtually every variety of Shaker product be explained? By what extraordinary process did the Shaker leadership arrive at such ideal designs from the contemporary standpoint? The answers to both questions must be unpalatable to people who believe in "doing your own thing." For it does seem likely that the reasons why Shaker design and Shaker skills achieved so high a level of simple excellence lay mainly in the harshness with which every devout Shaker repressed his or her personal impulses. The energy ordinary humans devoted to their private concerns was spent in every Shaker village on a ceaseless struggle toward selflessness.

Essentially, then, the Shaker artisan needed the rigor of this struggle to accomplish the marvels of Shaker craftsmanship. After the quest for perfect detachment gradually relaxed, the perfection of Shaker products also suffered. If life in the later-day Shaker villages was more peaceful than in Mother Lucy's era, it was more sterile, too. As the excitement of continuous warring against evil subsided, and more sedate forms of worship were adopted, Shakerism lost much of its appeal to emotion-starved converts—and it also lost most of its special artistry.

Yet there could be no doubt that the religion, at the peak of its fervor, had at least indirectly inspired a remarkable flowering of handcrafts. As far as most of the new admirers of Shakerism were concerned, the nuances of how and why the Shaker experiment had produced the contents of the new museums was not particularly important. The mere fact that a species of religious commune had created so much beauty seemed enough to justify attention, even by many young people who ordinarly might not enter another museum.

Besides, there was the matter of Shaker ingenuity. Didn't they invent the clothespin and the tilt-back chair and all manner of other simple devices for saving labor or healthfully increasing bodily comfort? For instance, Sister Sarah Babbitt of the Shaker settlement in Harvard, Massachusetts, "surprisingly" came up with the idea of the circular saw, probably around 1812, a pamphlet prepared by John Williams of Old Chatham tells visitors there.

In addition, the Shakers treated their women members in a more nearly equal fashion than was the case with society at large. The Shakers also put much stress on the importance of plain wholesome food as a health safeguard. They can even be said to have anticipated the back-to-the-earth movement prevalent among some young people today. They opposed war when pacifist sentiments were almost unheard of. Furthermore, they placed the highest possible value on religion, and they tried harder than practically any other people in recorded history to live up to an extremely rigid moral code.

For all these reasons, Shakerism would strike many new acquaintances as an extraordinary discovery. The most intense interest was stirred among the far-from-silent minority of Americans who were distressed by the direction the country appeared to be taking during the second half of the twentieth century. In their eyes, this small band of nineteenth-century idealists seemed uncannily relevant. For the Shakers had not just protested against a system they disliked, they had actually found a workable alternative. Or had they?

If there was one single rock (besides the question of celibacy) upon which the whole Shaker climb toward perfection had constantly faltered, it was the granite rigidity of the discipline it demanded of every believer. As early as the 1790's, cryptic references occur in Shaker records about the falling away from the faith by members refusing to obey their elders—and the main offenders, then and thereafter, were almost always from the age group that usually produces the most vigorous protesters. "I believe the late and present troubles among the young are the chief cause of my present weakness and suffering," Father Joseph wrote to Mother Lucy some time in 1794. Fifty years later, from her heavenly abode in the spirit world, Mother Lucy sent a special message to Shakers in their teens and early twenties. "If you ever get tired of being reproved and instructed by your Elders, and turn to the world for rest," she informed them, "you will have to go to hell. . . ."

But such threats did not prevent nearly all the young people brought up in the Shaker faith from running away at their first opportunity. Sometimes a lighter touch was tried to enforce the discipline the elders deemed essential, and yet sooner or later their orders had to be heeded, as indicated in a little story a mid-nineteenth-century visitor among the Shakers related:

> A youth in one of the Shaker settlements . . . was once asked whether he had his liberty and could do as he pleased. "Certainly," said the youth, "we do whatever we have a gift to." On being asked what he should do, if he wanted on a fine winter's morning to go and skate on Enfield pond, he replied, "I would tell the elder that I had a gift to go down and skate." Being asked further, whether the elder would probably permit him, he answered, "Certainly, unless the elder had a gift that I should not go." "But if you still told the elder that you had a gift to go down and skate, and go you must?" "Why then the elder would tell me that I had a 'lying gift' and he had a gift to beat me, if I did not go about my work immediately."

With the relaxing of other Shaker practices, the harshness of the Shaker discipline was also gradually eased. By 1920, Elder Nicholas Briggs, who had spent forty years among the Shakers before finally leaving in middle age, could ruefully write about his own youth at the Enfield community in New Hampshire. It was "like boarding school with no vacations," he said. But despite the relative freedom his own generation of Shakers had enjoyed, he still felt painful memories of having been subject to constant "dictation" by people no wiser than he was.

Was such experience really harmful? Devout Shakers, both past and present, would certainly deny it. In their view, to help any individual control his or her own will was to confer a blessing, not a punishment. "The true-souled and obedient Shaker is the freest person on the foot-stool of

God," Elder Harvey Eads of South Union in Kentucky once wrote, "because all his bonds are self-imposed."

Elder Harvey was the leading Shaker critic of the new directions Elder Frederick Evans set for Shakerism, and as the spokesman for Shakerism's conservative wing a century ago, he might be expected to defend the idea that the old-fashioned ways were best. Strangely enough, though, the same viewpoint has attracted some new disciples. For in addition to a revival of general interest in Shakerism during the past few decades, there has also been, more recently, a small but possibly growing movement toward reviving the religion itself. The leading figure in this movement is Theodore Johnson, the director of the library at the Sabbathday Lake community.

Mr. Johnson clearly has little patience with the calm attitude of defeat that characterized Shakerism during most of the present century. Ever since the two eldresses of New Lebanon had published a sort of lament for their religion back in 1905, the serene old ladies representing the last remaining Shakers had been telling sympathetic outsiders not to grieve for them. From the vast stock of sayings attributed to Mother Ann, they had drawn a few sentences that made them feel sure Shakerism had not really failed. A time might come when only a handful of Shakers would have trouble burying their dead, Mother Ann was supposed to have predicted. But that would still be no sign that evil had triumphed over good. Eventually the faith would be reborn and would prevail.

Mr. Johnson would very much like to emphasize the last part of Mother Ann's prediction, although he does insist that he wants to avoid any controversy with those remaining women at Canterbury who decreed an end to all Shaker recruiting in 1964. Nevertheless, he willingly describes his own hopes for the future.

"Even within the last three or four months, ten or a dozen people have come knocking very seriously on our door here," he reports. One is a public-school teacher drawn to the Shaker way of life since first reading about the religion in college. Another is an insurance man, still another an engineer for a radio station. While this new wave of prospective recruits probably includes more men than women, a young woman currently teaching English on a college campus would certainly qualify as a serious candidate. "And two young ladies who run a nursery school in Vermont would come tomorrow."

Mr. Johnson, a vigorous man of middle years, scoffs at the suggestion that any of these applicants might be to some extent motivated by the hope of sharing in a division of valuable Shaker assets if they joined a small society composed mainly of much older people. "If the door is not opened," he explains, "the assets would be turned over to a corporation already formed to preserve the property as a museum."

Two other reasons had been put forward, though, when the Canterbury decision to stop recruiting was announced. After the death of Brother Delmer Wilson, there was no longer any male Shaker to instruct new brothers. And in Canterbury's opinion, young people seeking admittance would not be capable of observing the basic Shaker rule of celibacy.

Both of these reasons, according to Mr. Johnson, were irrational. "The society here is anxious to take new members," he declares. "Canterbury says, 'You may not have them.' " But when and if this prohibition is repealed, several dozen recruits would immediately appear—"at least half of them within twenty-four hours."

Will it happen? Will Shakerism really be revived? Who can say?

Shaker Museums and
Public Collections*

While the following list is included mainly for the benefit of those who would like to see authentic Shaker products, it may also help students with research into some aspects of the Shaker experience. However, as indicated in various chapters of this book, the great number of requests for help has made it difficult for the limited staffs of Shaker museums to provide the requested assistance. It is strongly suggested that any appeal, whether in person or by mail, be made as specific as possible. If you just ask for "material about the Shakers," the response is likely to be unhelpful. But if you specify that it is Shaker music, or Shaker furniture, or Shaker religious beliefs that particularly concerns you, many of the following may be able to send you useful pamphlets or reprints of Shaker documents. Nevertheless, the Suggestions for Further Reading on page 207 will probably prove more helpful to most students.

DELAWARE

Henry Francis DuPont Winterthur Museum, Winterthur 19735

Off State Rte. 52. Shaker storage walls, furniture,

* This list is based on the 1973 Guide to Shaker Museums and Libraries prepared by Robert F. W. Meader, director of the Shaker Museum at Old Chatham, New York, whose generosity in permitting such use of his material is hereby acknowledged.

baskets, and fabrics displayed in a re-created dwelling room and storage room. The two rooms may be seen on museum tours, for which reservations are required. Museum closed first two weeks in July and on national holidays. Fee. Tel. (302) 656 8591

KENTUCKY

Kentucky Museum, Bowling Green 42101

Kentucky Building, Rte. U.S. 68 on Western Kentucky University campus. Collection of Kentuckiana, including South Union Shaker furniture, tools, and crafts. Monday–Friday, 9–5; Saturday, 9–4; Sunday, 2–4. No fee. Tel. (502) 745 2592

**Shakertown at Pleasant Hill, Inc., Harrodsburg 40330

Rte. U.S. 68, 25 miles southwest of Lexington. A restored Shaker village, of which 27 original buildings remain; finest Shaker collection in the South. Dining and overnight lodgings available in original buildings. Daily, 9–5. Fee. Tel. (606) 734 9111

**Shakertown at South Union 42283

Rte. U.S. 68, 15 miles west of Bowling Green. A large collection of Shaker furniture, crafts, and inventions housed in former Shaker buildings. May 1–October 15. Monday–Saturday, 9–5, Sunday, 1–5. During the winter, by appointment, for groups. Fee. Tel. (502) 542 4167; winter (502) 542 4720

MAINE

**Shaker Museum, Sabbathday Lake Shaker Community, Poland Spring 04274

** Museum devoted exclusively to Shaker artifacts.

Rte. 26, 8 miles north of Exit 11, Maine Turnpike, at Gray. An original Shaker village founded in 1793, still occupied by Shaker sisters. Gift shop sells Shaker-made items and is open year round, Sundays excepted; museum open to visitors May 30–October 1, Tuesday–Saturday, 10–4:30. Closed Sunday, Monday. Fee. Tel. (207) 926 4391

MASSACHUSETTS
Boston Museum of Fine Arts, Boston 02115
465 Huntington Ave. Re-created Shaker room with furniture, artifacts. Tuesday–Sunday, 10–5; Tuesday evenings until 9. Closed Mondays, Thanksgiving, Christmas, New Year's Day, July 4. Fee except Tuesday evening and no fee for children under 16. Tel. (617) 267 9300

**Fruitlands Museums, Harvard 01451
Rte. 110 north of village. One of five museums on the grounds, the Shaker house (moved from Harvard Shaker community) contains furniture and other items largely from Harvard community. May 30–September 30, Tuesday–Sunday, 1–5. Fee. Tel. (617) 456 3924

**Hancock Shaker Community, Inc., Hancock 01201
Rte. U.S. 20, 5 miles west of Pittsfield. A former Shaker village now largely restored; 17 original buildings, including famous Round Barn. Shaker furniture, artifacts, industrial exhibits. June 1–October 15, daily 9:30–5. Fee. Tel. (413) 443 0188

NEW HAMPSHIRE
**Canterbury Shaker Museum, East Canterbury 03224
Thirteen miles northeast of Concord off Rte. 106. An

original Shaker village founded in 1792, still occupied
by Shaker sisters. Gift shop sells Shaker-made items.
May 30–Labor Day, Tuesday–Saturday, tours on the
hour, 9–4. Closed Sunday, Monday. Fee. Tel. (603)
783 6312

NEW YORK

**Shaker Museum, Old Chatham 12136

Off Rte. 66, 5 miles from exit B-2 of Berkshire Spur
of N.Y. Thruway. Oldest and largest museum devoted
to Shaker crafts; 36 galleries housing 18,000 objects.
May 1–October 31 daily, 10–5:30. Fee. Tel. (518)
757 2063

OHIO

Dunham Tavern Museum, Cleveland 44106

6709 Euclid Ave. Re-created Shaker room. Daily all
year, 12:30–4:30, except Monday and holidays. No
fee. Tel. (216) 431 1060

Golden Lamb Hotel, Lebanon 45036

27–31 South Broadway, on Rte. 63 between I-71 and
1-75. Ohio's oldest hotel, richly furnished with antiques, many Shaker items. Authentic Shaker bed-
room and Shaker dining room for the public. No fee.
Tel. (513) 932 5065

Shaker Historical Society Museum, Shaker Heights
44120

16740 South Park Blvd. Shaker furniture, crafts, industries, largely from North Union community. Tuesday–Friday, 2–4; Sunday, 2–5; closed Monday and
Saturday. No fee. Tel. (216) 921 1201

Warren County Historical Society Museum, Lebanon
45036

105 South Broadway, on Rte. 63 between I-71 and I-75. Shaker furniture and crafts largely from Union village displayed in one room and one gallery. Tuesday–Saturday, 9–4; Sunday, 12–4. Fee. Tel. (513) 932 1817

Western Reserve Historical Society, Cleveland 44106
10825 East Blvd. Shaker furniture, crafts, inventions displayed in the Shaker Room. Tuesday–Saturday, 10–5; Sunday, 2–5. Closed on national holidays. No fee. Tel. (216) 721 5722

PENNSYLVANIA

Philadelphia Museum of Art, Philadelphia 19130
Benjamin Franklin Parkway at 26th St. Exhibit of Shaker furniture, artifacts. Daily 9–5. Closed on national holidays. Fee except Sunday mornings and Mondays. Tel. (215) 763 8100

VERMONT

Shelburne Museum, Shelburne 05482
Rte. U.S. 7, seven miles south of Burlington. Shaker artifacts in Shaker shed from Canterbury, N.H. May 15–October 15. Daily, 9–5. Fee. Tel. (802) 985 3344

WISCONSIN

Milwaukee Art Centre, Milwaukee 53202
2220 North Terrace Ave. Wednesday, Saturday, Sunday, 1–5; closed holidays. July and August, Wednesday–Sunday, 1–5. No fee. Tel. (414) 271 9508

Suggestions for Further Reading

THE PERFECT LIFE *is based on a wide variety of Shaker manuscripts and old books that are not generally available. As indicated on p.* 201, *pamphlets and reprints of old documents about specific aspects of Shakerism may be secured from some of these institutions; and for students who wish to delve more deeply into some phase of Shakerism, copies of* The Shaker Quarterly, *subscribed to by large public libraries, may be most helpful. The following reading list is intended only to suggest some sources that can be more easily obtained.*

ANDREWS, EDWARD DEMING, *The People Called Shakers.* New York, Oxford University Press, 1953. Paperback, New York, Dover, 1963.

———, *The Gift to Be Simple.* New York, J. J. Augustin, 1940. Paperback, New York, Dover, 1962.

——— and FAITH ANDREWS, *Shaker Furniture.* New Haven, Yale University Press, 1937. Paperback, New York, Dover, 1950.

MELCHER, MARGUERITE FELLOWS, *The Shaker Adventure.* Princeton, Princeton University Press, 1941. Paperback, Cleveland, Press of Case Western Reserve University, 1968.

MORSE, FLO, *Yankee Communes.* New York, Harcourt Brace Jovanovich, 1971.

NORDHOFF, CHARLES, *The Communistic Societies of the United States*. Paperback, New York, Schocken, 1965.

NOYES, JOHN HUMPHREY, *Strange Cults and Utopias of 19th Century America* (originally published in 1870 as *History of American Socialisms*). Paperback, New York, Dover, 1966.

VOSS, CARL HERMANN, *In Search of Meaning: Living Religions of the World*. Cleveland, World Publishing Company, 1968.

Index